Praise for
Honest to God Prayer:
Spirituality as Awareness, Empowerment,
Relinquishment and Paradox

"Groff blurs the line between the folks who are religious and folks who claim spirituality by mining truths in a variety of traditions and offering them to us in story, insight and poetry. Honest to God ... I love it!"
—**Nancy Corcoran, CSJ**, author, *Secrets of Prayer: A Multifaith Guide to Creating Personal Prayer in Your Life;* Catholic chaplain, Wellesley College

"Will enrich people active in their faith traditions as well as the growing number of people describing themselves as spiritual but not religious. Helps you see God in all things and all things in God."
—**Bruce Epperly**, author, *Tending to the Holy: The Practice of the Presence of God in Ministry* and *Holy Adventure: 41 Days of Audacious Living*

"Remind[s] us that prayer has its own movement and rhythm which we can learn to follow.... Weaves together the wisdom to be learned from the seasons of the day, Ignatian prayer and Native American spirituality in ways that respect the integrity of each, but where each is enriched by the other.... Offers the reader a multiplicity of concrete ways to pray that are both ancient and fresh, [and] an enlivening vision in a sometimes tired field of spirituality volumes."
—**Christine Valters Paintner, PhD**, author, *Desert Fathers and Mothers: Early Christian Wisdom Sayings—Annotated & Explained* and *Lectio Divina—The Sacred Art: Transforming Words & Images into Heart-Centered Prayer*

"A most excellent presentation of prayer as a wholly different mind and a renewed heart, much more than mere verbal recitations or formulas.... Offers you a truly larger house to live in, and a house that will not confine you, but one filled with doors and windows—and plenty of skylight."
—**Fr. Richard Rohr, OFM**, Center for Action and Contemplation, Albuquerque, New Mexico; author, *Falling Upward* and *The Naked Now*

"A rich and in-depth exploration of the ongoing expression of prayer in our spiritual journeys [and] an extraordinary resource for all seekers—from those who have well-established prayer practices to those for whom prayer is something new—who are spiritual but not religious. Easy to read yet filled with profound insights that inspire a deeper relationship with Source."
  —**Kay Lindahl**, founder of The Listening Center; author, *The Sacred Art of Listening: Forty Reflections for Cultivating a Spiritual Practice;* and other books

"A sublime spiritual companion on the path toward a life of empowered, authentic prayer. Shares from the wisdom of a variety of faith traditions [and] equips us to embrace a truly awakened spiritual life—the kind we've always dreamed of and prayed for."
  —**The Rev. Peter M. Wallace**, host of *Day1;* author, *The Passionate Jesus: What We Can Learn from Jesus about Love, Fear, Grief, Joy and Living Authentically*

"[A] wonderful trailbreaker on the spiritual life.... If you pray for stuff, don't read this book. If you pray for wisdom, read it twice."
  —**Rabbi Rami Shapiro**, author, *The Sacred Art of Lovingkindness: Preparing to Practice;* and other books

"If you yearn for real-life spiritual renewal, this book is for you! Wherever you open these pages, you will find resources, guidance, grace and honest companionship for your own prayerful journey."
  —**Heidi Neumark**, Lutheran pastor; author, *Breathing Space: A Spiritual Journey in the South Bronx*

"Opens the curtains on a new perspective, enabling the sunlight of a new way to break in.... Rubs the eyes of tired ecclesia and provides plentiful resources toward discarding unnecessary angst. Here is a holistic guidebook for prayer, particularly for those who haven't got a prayer."
  —**Scott Burton**, minister of St. Matthew's Church, Perth, Scotland; author, *Holy Whitewater: Reflections on the Spirituality of Kayaking*

"Lively and packed with wisdom from many traditions.... Offers a rich feast of possibilities for weaving prayer through daily life. I found myself marking page after page with a resounding, 'Yes!'"
  —**Nancy L. Bieber**, author, *Decision Making & Spiritual Discernment: The Sacred Art of Finding Your Way*

HONEST
to God
PRAYER

Spirituality as Awareness, Empowerment, Relinquishment and Paradox

Kent Ira Groff

Walking Together, Finding the Way®
SKYLIGHT PATHS®
PUBLISHING
Woodstock, Vermont

Honest to God Prayer:
Spirituality as Awareness, Empowerment, Relinquishment and Paradox

2013 Quality Paperback Edition, First Printing
© 2013 Kent Ira Groff

For information regarding permission to reprint material from this book, please write or fax your request to SkyLight Paths Publishing, Permissions Department, at the address / fax number listed below, or e-mail your request to permissions@skylightpaths.com.

Unless otherwise indicated, scripture quotations are from the *New Revised Standard Version Bible*, © 1989 by the Division of Christian Education of the National Council of the Churches of Christ in the USA. Used by permission. All rights reserved.

Scripture quotations noted as AT refer to Author's Translation of the text based on the original languages in Hebrew or Greek.

Scripture quotations from interfaith traditions, unless otherwise noted, are from *World Scripture: A Comparative Anthology of Sacred Texts*, ed. by Andrew Wilson (St. Paul: Paragon House, 1995).

Poetry, unless otherwise noted, is that of the author © Kent Ira Groff. Some poems and brief portions of *Honest to God Prayer* are adapted from the author's previous writings © Kent Ira Groff.

First names used in brief stories or quotations are not the actual name of the persons.

Library of Congress Cataloging-in-Publication Data

Groff, Kent Ira.
  Honest to God prayer : spirituality as awareness, empowerment, relinquishment and paradox : an interfaith weaving of Native American and Ignatian spiritual themes / Kent Ira Groff.
    p. cm. — (Walking together, finding the way)
  Includes bibliographical references and index.
  ISBN 978-1-59473-433-5 (pbk.)
  1. Prayer. 2. Spirituality. 3. Ignatius of Loyola, Saint, 1491-1556. Exercitia spiritualia. 4. Indians of North America—Religion. 5. Ignatius, of Loyola, Saint, 1491-1556. I. Title.
  BL560.G755 2012
  248.3'2—dc23

                                    2012034248

10 9 8 7 6 5 4 3 2 1

Manufactured in the United States of America

Cover & Interior Design: Tim Holtz
Cover Image: © Elena Elisseeva/Shutterstock

SkyLight Paths, "Walking Together, Finding the Way," and colophon are trademarks of LongHill Partners, Inc., registered in the U.S. Patent and Trademark Office.

Walking Together, Finding the Way®
Published by SkyLight Paths Publishing
A Division of LongHill Partners, Inc.
Sunset Farm Offices, Route 4, P.O. Box 237
Woodstock, VT 05091
Tel: (802) 457-4000 Fax: (802) 457-4004
www.skylightpaths.com

Contents

Index of Prayer Practices

Theme III: Practices for Cultivating Relinquishment

Theme IV: Practices for Cultivating Paradox

Orientation

What is prayer? And how does prayer relate to spirituality? *Pray* can seem like such a religious word that many people may view it as a cliché or dismiss it. So I suggest that to pray is to yearn for something beyond ourselves, and prayer in its many forms is how we express that yearning. I often say, tell me your yearnings and I'll tell you your prayers.

Religiously motivated people, on the other hand, may know how to pray—they may have memorized certain words, patterns, or methods. However, prayer is an ongoing, transforming process, not a technique. And the fruit of genuine praying is to yearn for bits and pieces of passion and compassion in all of life—in its grit and grace.

We have just landed on a beginning definition of spirituality: the fruit of genuine, honest to God prayer expressed in our relationships in all of life.

By honest to God praying I mean cultivating that intentional yearning or longing to discover traces of passion and compassion in the most heart-wrenching suffering, and in the heart-rewarding successes of life. If the goal of prayer is to lead to genuine spirituality in all circumstances, then, as the saying goes, the way there is to practice, practice, practice.

We might say, then, that prayer is the practice route that leads to the fruit of a passionate and compassionate spiritual life. Spirituality is not a thing you can put in your pocket, but a genuine lived experience of giving and receiving love in all the twists and turns of your journey.

How *Honest to God Prayer* Evolved: Four Themes

What I offer here is a compass with four directional themes to survey varied stages of your journey. The four movements of prayer in this little book have been gestating for two decades: waking up to reality (awareness), claiming gifts (empowerment), practicing detachment in success and failure (relinquishment), and experiencing mystery (paradox). While developing these four themes, I began to see connections to prayer in four directions in Native American tradition and the four movements or "weeks" in Ignatian spirituality, which I refer to throughout this book (see "Prologue" and "Bring It All Together").

Awareness marks the beginning movement of prayer in spiritual streams of East and West: to wake up to reality, to pay attention in the morning of life, open to its potential and pain. You keep waking up to begin again, all your life.

A second movement of prayer is *empowerment*: to embrace your dreams and possibilities in the noon of life, claiming your gifts. Even though claiming power may sound a bit self-serving, honest to God prayer means knocking until a door of opportunity opens for you to use your gifts. And that process of knocking can teach humility.

A third movement of prayer is *relinquishment*: the great letting-go process of detachment in the afternoon of life, emptying your agenda—or it's emptied for you. Even though relinquishing may sound a bit self-denying, unless you practice detachment you are not free to receive the next gift.

As a fourth movement, prayer as *paradox* weds seeming opposites in the night of life: here is the mystery. Prayer becomes a dance that integrates simplicity and complexity, claiming and relinquishing childlike dreams in abilities and disabilities, giving and receiving compassion, living actively and contemplatively—alone yet all one.

The four movements or themes are not always sequential, and you may cycle back and forth in your life experience—and in this book. As in a tapestry, a weaver may introduce a bright amber thread into a primarily turquoise background but create a whole amber section later on. So, for example, I may introduce a small thread that speaks of relinquishment in a chapter that's about empowerment, while saving the primary message of relinquishment for the chapter on emptying.

In another sense, this book began evolving five decades ago, when Bishop John A. T. Robinson's classic bestseller *Honest to God* ushered the Copernican revolution into our everyday language and views of God. Instead of a God "up there" or "out there," Robinson drew on twentieth-century theologian Paul Tillich's idea of God as the Ground of our being—as depth in every sphere of life. In *Honest to God Prayer* I aim to integrate such *ideas* about God with your *experience* of God as grounding through the process of practicing prayer.

> Prayer is the practice route that leads to the fruit of a passionate and compassionate spiritual life.

Grounding and Process for Each Theme

First, for each of these four movements, I offer a chapter that surveys the *grounding*. Here I draw on sacred texts and concepts in varied spiritual traditions and cultural wisdom related to each theme: awareness, empowerment, relinquishment, and paradox.

Second comes a chapter on *process*, where I explore hands-on ways of living into each of the four movements. I have a passion to link ancient traditions with lived experience. You might say the grounding is more focused on *spirituality* and left-brain history and ideas, whereas the process has more to do with *prayer* and right-brain experience and lived life.

At the end of each theme, I invite you to engage in *prayer practices* as a laboratory for experiencing each theme. Prayer is to spirituality as the laboratory is to science, the place of experimentation and application. Prayer is like a chemistry lab where you experiment with a quandary to discover an aha! Prayer is like an archeological dig inviting you to discover buried treasures. You may go for long periods without discoveries—or find something you aren't looking for in the grit by surprise.

How This Book Can Work for You

Honest to God Prayer is interactive, offering grist for personal and group reflection, along with prayer practices that can enrich you any way you read it:

- ∽ For personal and spiritual growth and formation;
- ∽ As a devotional enrichment tool, garnering little bits at a time, not always sequentially;
- ∽ As an opening meditation with a group, or board, or committee, using a prayer practice or a brief quotation;
- ∽ For nurturing spiritual friendship, by reading and sharing with another person, perhaps of a different faith tradition;
- ∽ For short-term classes in your faith community, or as a resource for an interfaith group;
- ∽ As a resource for planning a retreat, or for a series of mini-retreats;
- ∽ As a curriculum resource for academic classes or training programs in spiritual direction or formation.

Notes on Keeping a Journal

Any way you use this book, you can sharpen the eyes of your perception by keeping a journal. Why keep a journal? And how?

Journaling is a way to listen to your own story-journey and make sense out of fragmented experiences. Reflect on the meaning of the word *journal* itself. Using a *jour*nal helps to integrate each isolated *jour* (day) with the process of your lifelong *jour*ney. Your fingers create a connection between your head and your heart.

Journal longhand, or use your computer. By reflecting through your fingertips on an "Aha!" or an "Aargh!" moment, you create the grounding for the next awareness in the process of your journey. Back and forth it goes, the paradox of grounding and process.

I joke about making only two rules for journaling. First, date each entry. Second, make a mistake in the first entry. That's because the biggest barrier to journaling is being too self-critical, writing out of the head instead of the heart. Another barrier is missed days—so aim for four days out of seven, or find your own rhythm. These prayer practices are designed to link critical thinking and creative imagination—good grist for journaling.

Once a student bounded up to me, just as I was ready to begin teaching, and asked, "What is spirituality?" I turned to the class, and this is what we came up with: *Spirituality is learning to respond rather than react to the circumstances of your life and to the events of the world, in such a way that blesses your own soul and the world.*

> Spirituality is learning to respond rather than react to the circumstances of your life and to the events of the world, in such a way that blesses your own soul and the world.

Prayer fuels our yearning for God and creates experiential methods for the Spirit in that transformative learning process. Keeping a journal is one more such method.

Interfaith Connections

In returning now to this book that's been incubating for two decades, I've become aware of deeper interfaith connections. In the years between, I've traveled, led retreats, companioned spiritual seekers and leaders, and integrated varied spiritual traditions in my books *What Would I Believe If I Didn't Believe Anything?* and *Facing East, Praying West*. I've had time to see both overlapping and contrasting threads in unique spiritual traditions. I surely don't want to homogenize unique texts and textures of particular religions. Such contrasting and even clashing colors need to be honored in ever-expanding tapestries.

To shift the metaphor, the more deeply each of us drinks from our own well, the more we discover that we're connected by a common underground stream of compassionate yearning—which is prayer. So in these pages, I try to interweave and juxtapose interfaith spiritual sources. I hope I do this with integrity, while honoring both the depth and breadth of my own Christian well.

Honest to God Prayer: Grace in the Grit

Reality is bittersweet. On the wall beside me I'm looking at metal sand castings, made by my son in middle school, representing the ancient faces of comedy and tragedy. Life is full of blessings and brokenness, the one often filtered through the other. Our idealistic dreams soon clash with practical and political realities. We have to eke out a livelihood yet still long for meaning and purpose through our work. We cherish intimacy, yet our closest relationships cause the deepest pain.

> Genuine praying is not an escape from disturbing realities, but rather a whole-hearted embracing of life's ambiguities.

What the old miners in Colorado, where I live, called "pay dirt," provides an apt metaphor for our experience of the spiritual life: only by paying attention to the dirt will we ever see any flecks of gold. Sometimes all we seem to see is dirt. When we do find gold, it usually surfaces through some combination of the surprise grin of circumstances and the long-term grit of our own and others' toil and sufferings.

Here's the key to grounding honest to God prayer: genuine praying is not an escape from disturbing realities, but rather a wholehearted embracing of life's ambiguities. If we frame prayer this way, it becomes the laboratory for noticing sacred particulars in secular stuff. We may be pounded and dazzled and astonished and beaten and illuminated and humbled in the very same experience.

Grit Seasoning

While I do this grit
work, season
the irksome pieces
with enough
Ahas! to remind me
of the reason.

Prologue

Integrating Native American and Ignatian Spiritual Streams

In the early 1990s, I began practicing a form of Native American prayer facing the four directions that parallel the four themes of this book: the East as the morning of childlike curiosity; the South as the noon energies of passion and vocation; the West as the afternoon of letting go; the North as the night of depth and mystery.[1] I recognize the risk in borrowing others' sacred treasures. Yet it also honors another's tradition, as Native teachers tell me, if you draw from it with respect and integrity in ways that connect with lost parts of your own soul's ancient core, in my case, with Celtic spirituality. It's my prayer that modern people keep alive primal directions of nature to honor the stages of our journey at each compass point: from childhood to midlife to eldering to dying.

I've also become aware, since making the month-long Ignatian retreat in India, how the four movements or "weeks" of Ignatius's *Spiritual Exercises* in many ways parallel the four directions and themes of this book: prayer as awareness, empowerment, relinquishment, and paradox.[2] The Ignatian way, from Catholic tradition, seeks to unite action and contemplation with imagination to discern how best to love. Is that not the way of Christ? Is that not the goal of Benedictine, Quaker, or any authentic spiritual path of East or West, North or South? Is it not to practice uniting the inner and outer life that we can say with Gandhi, "My life is my message"?

This brief synopsis will prepare you as I weave Native American and Ignatian parallels in the four themes of the book.

Theme I: Awareness

Facing the East at sunrise represents childhood as the morning of life in Native primal traditions, and corresponds to the first movement of prayer as awareness. Like the season of spring, each day the rising sun bids us to begin anew by restoring the wounded yet creative child within, to move forward with curiosity for new adventure.

> We are both small and great, mortals created for the divine purpose of living fully awake and alive to love.

In Ignatius's *Spiritual Exercises*, the first movement focuses on the awareness that life is beautiful yet also broken. Attentiveness to divine love calls you to return to your original blessing—as a unique person, yet one with all creation. Paralleling the East in Native tradition, Anthony de Mello, SJ, a Jesuit guru from India, often said, "In the first week, let the child in you come forth." In both Native and Ignatian spiritual streams, the theme of awareness calls us to awaken to an ancient truth: that we are both small and great, mortals created for the divine purpose of living fully awake and alive to love.

Theme II: Empowerment

Facing the South represents the noon of life, fertility, healing, and abundance in Native spirituality. Like the season of summer, it is a time for growth, for focus upward on discovering and living out your passion and vision, for creatively using your vocational and sexual energies for the good of the earth.

Prayer as empowerment parallels the second movement of *The Spiritual Exercises*, with its focus on incarnation, embodied Love in the world, as seen in the life of Jesus's powerful message and actions. As Ignatius invites the use of imagination in prayer, especially in scenes from Gospel stories, you can transfer your use of imagination to all of life. Like the direction of the South, the second movement culminates in an exercise for discerning life choices to fulfill your vocational purpose (see "Choosing Well, Living Whole" at the end of chapter four).

Theme III: Relinquishment

Facing the West represents the afternoon of life in Native spirituality, the time for embracing the shadow and inner wisdom of the self. Like the season of fall with leaves changing colors, the power of the sun wanes and yet its beauty waxes. By embracing diminishments, you cultivate detachment from the world of materialism. You recognize your connection to all creation, releasing hurts and practicing forgiveness, with deepening wisdom in rhythm with ancient rocks and rivers.

> By embracing diminishments, you cultivate detachment from the world of materialism.

Prayer as relinquishment parallels the third movement of *The Spiritual Exercises*, with its focus on Jesus's suffering and crucifixion, representing the spiritual theme of the dying to the ego to find new life. The message of Jesus is about dying to what is false, about detaching from things in order to live joyfully and wholly alive in the Spirit in the now and then of eternal life. Jesus's words from the cross echo our sense of forsakenness and our need for forgiveness, so that we live and die with purpose: "It is finished." Paralleling the Native direction of the West and its rhythm with creation, the Gospels tell us that when Jesus died all creation was affected as darkness fell on the land, the earth shook, and rocks split.

Theme IV: Paradox

Facing the North is associated with the ancestors in Native tradition, and as such it bids us to the paradox of connecting ancient primal traditions with our life in the modern technological world. It is the time when we glimpse the vast depths and beauty of the universe, inwardly aware of wisdom far beyond ourselves. Like the season of winter, which is for primal peoples a time for storytelling, the nighttime constellations convey ancient stories and myths and offer direction in life's night.

> Through prayer, we experience the paradoxical union of life's polarities in the Lord of Life.

In each of the directions you honor the sky above and the earth beneath in union with each compass point within yourself. Here is the Mystery of the integrative life.

In Ignatius's *Spiritual Exercises*, the fourth movement focuses on resurrection, which I translate as "resilient Love." Resurrection happens whenever life knocks you down and you bounce back with gratitude and compassion. Love rises and explodes into new life in us, like the stars in the cosmos as we join God's purpose. Through prayer, we experience the paradoxical union of life's polarities in the Lord of Life: present while absent, speaking while silent, moving while still. Like the mystery of light, the wave and particle are one.

Prayer as Awareness

Opening

CHAPTER ONE

Waking Up to Reality

The Grounding for Awareness

Prayer means turning to Reality.
—EVELYN UNDERHILL

We have two or three great moving experiences in
our lives—experiences so great and so moving that it
doesn't seem at the time anyone else has been so caught
up and pounded and dazzled and astonished and beaten
and broken and rescued and illuminated and rewarded
and humbled in just that way ever before.
—F. SCOTT FITZGERALD

*A*wareness *is the beginning, middle, and end of every major stream of*
spirituality: listen, wake up, pay attention. A rabbi friend tells
me that the burning bush was not the real miracle, but rather that
Moses "turned aside to see" (Exodus 3:3–4). The Hebrew word for
"turn" is *shuv* (often translated in religious language moralistically
as "repent"): simple turning creates spiritual awareness. That's why

twentieth-century Christian mystic Evelyn Underhill says, "Prayer means turning to Reality"—because Reality includes the mundane and the sacred. Real prayer begins with simple turning to what is, opening to awareness, then seeing more than meets the eye.

The direction for awakening in primal and biblical traditions is the East, and its time is dawn. The name Buddha means "one who is awake," and the disciple's goal is to live awake, to cultivate the practice of awareness, mindfulness. The Buddhist practice of *maranasati* or "death meditation" encourages persons to encounter the awareness of their own death in order to live fully in this life. Many who have cancer or HIV or near-death experiences have awakened to living into each day as a precious gift.

> What's really important to you that you need to wake up to?

Brushes with death shake you awake to see again with the eyes of a child. In the Christian Gospels, just before Jesus is to die, he paints a landscape of personal, political, and global catastrophes, each punctuated with the refrain, "Keep awake" (see Mark 13). The Apostle Paul writes, "Set your minds on things that are above, not on things that are on earth, for you have died and your life is hidden with Christ in God" (Colossians 3:3). Likewise in *The Spiritual Exercises*, Ignatius of Loyola invites you to contemplate a wise and good choice by visualizing yourself on your deathbed.

It's not just a religious theory. "Remembering that I'll be dead soon is the most important tool I've ever encountered to help me make the big choices in life," said Apple's cofounder Steve Jobs to Stanford University graduates in 2005—six years before he died. "Because almost everything—all external expectations, all pride, all fear of embarrassment or failure—these things just fall away in the face of death, leaving only what is truly important."[1]

What's really important to you that you need to wake up to? You don't need to wait until you're fifty, or until a career implodes or a marriage dies.

Life is ultimately defined by what you pay attention to. What you focus on feeds you—my translation of nineteenth-century German philosopher Ludwig Feuerbach's idea that "man is what he eats." Genuine prayer doesn't just focus on sweetness and light, but also finds grist for growth by reflecting on struggles, diminishments, even wrong turns. Because once we become aware of the wrong turn, we've already turned our thoughts toward Reality.

> Prayer means paying attention to traces of grace in the grit, and if we suppress the grit we miss the grace.

Prayer means paying attention to traces of grace in the grit, and if we suppress the grit we miss the grace. The most important Hebrew prayer is the *Shema*, named for the first word, meaning *hear*, *listen*, or *pay attention*. "Listen, O Israel: the Lord our God is one" (Deuteronomy 6:4, AT). Deep listening draws us into loving oneness with God, neighbor, and self, as Jesus reaffirmed (Matthew 22:37–38).

Listen to Love, to love. *Shema* bids you to attentiveness with all your soul, your whole being—heart, will, mind, and body. Mindfulness expresses this contemplative listening in Eastern spirituality, for which the tree offers a primal unifying metaphor.

The Tree of Life: Paradigm of Outward and Inward Awareness

The tree stands as a paradigm of the spiritual life in the Hebrew Bible and Christian Scriptures and in scores of indigenous traditions.[2] From the milk-yielding agave tree of the Aztecs to the gigantic baobab of East Africa to the ancient Chinese ginkgo to the sacred lotus in Asia to the sycamore, hallowed by the Romans, who watered its roots with wine, the tree of life stands as a primal spiritual metaphor of the undivided life.

The Hebrew Bible begins in Genesis with the tree of life in the middle of a garden. The fruit-bearing tree by streams of water represents persons for whom life is integrated: "they meditate day and night" (Psalm 1:2–3). Christian Scriptures conclude with the tree of life in the middle of the city with its leaves "for the healing of the nations" (Revelation 22:2). The tree stands as a healing image of prayer at the center of every layer of environment: rural and urban, personal and global, spiritual and political.

As a model for the personal spiritual life, imagine the upper part of the tree as a *manifestation* of our life of action, bearing fruit in the world, risking stresses of wind and weather. Imagine the root system as the hidden life of *contemplation*, resting beneath conscious awareness. The trunk—interacting with earth and sky—represents attention (*shema*): listening attentively to the Ground of our being cultivates our listening attentively in the world of action. Yet the tree is one, signifying a union of outward and inward attention, and both are prayer.

Horticultural science dispels the simplistic idea that the roots nurture the tree. In reality, the vital feeding takes place in the interaction between the secluded root system and the visible leaves—in the complex process of photosynthesis (we'll explore "simplexity" in the final theme of paradox).[3] So the underground life of contemplative prayer nurtures us through the interaction with our active, visible life in the world. Noticing events in the world calls us to inner reflection. You can contemplate the beauty of a rosebud or the anguish of a car crash and notice your soul's response.

The tree of life invites you to notice and offer the "what is" of your unique personality type. Like the hickory with its deep roots, perhaps you are more of an introverted solitary type; or, like the aspen and sequoia, with spreading roots that intertwine, maybe you are more of an extraverted communal personality.

On yet another level, evergreens correspond to even-keel, steady, dependable personality types (like my wife), while deciduous trees correspond to creative, artistic persons—sometimes with wild mood swings and seasons (like myself). Which is better? In these poetic lines, I answer both—the evergreen *and* the one that sheds its leaves: December's tree is linked with Jesus's birth, and Friday's barren tree with budding Easter mirth.

The lotus tree expresses this "Easter" truth in Buddhist spirituality: that even wasted experiences can morph into new life. A Buddhist scripture says, "A sweet-smelling, lovely lotus may grow upon a heap of rubbish thrown by the highway" (Dhammapada 58–59). And where is Jesus crucified? On a tree at Golgotha, the town garbage heap.

Buddhist and Christian metaphors speak the same reality: that new life rises out of the garbage. A woman on silent retreat was praying when she heard a construction worker say, "Holy shit!" Later she and I pondered: Can this pop-culture phrase mask our human yearning for life's "waste" to become a source of wholeness and holiness? Maybe people are "praying" without knowing it—that life's lowest places might be consecrated: "Holy humus!" The expression can mean more than venting your spleen. By meditating with the "what is" of our experiences, we begin to see traces of grace rising from the grit of our own or others' defeats and discouragements. If we ignore the real stuff of life we miss Reality.

Leaving

> A leaf that has served its function
> as a thing of beauty
> can only become
> nurturing
> humus
> when it
> leaves:
> detaching
> as it grieves,
> it fails and falls
> to the Ground of its being
> to nurture another thing of beauty.

The image of God as the "Ground of being," from fifteenth-century mystic Meister Eckhart and popularized by twentieth-century theologian Paul Tillich, offers an alternative metaphor of the Divine—from a God out there or up there, to God within the earthy ballast of our experience. Prayer is what you do to get your own ground ready— to use an image of nineteenth-century Danish philosopher Søren Kierkegaard. As the tree of life shows us, prayer is a way of being rooted and grounded in love. Centering prayer offers a practical method for this grounding in the tree of life (see Prayer Practice 4).

Psalms: A Template for Praying "What Is"

Where can you go to find your unvarnished thoughts and feelings validated when you may have no words? The Psalms in Jewish-Christian tradition present bare-bones reality as the surest lens for praying and waking up to the Presence in the real world. In poetic and musical form, these prayers offer raw, uncensored yearnings to God (see Prayer Practice 1).

The first Psalm in the Hebrew Bible's prayer book opens with the metaphor of the tree, as we noted. It describes the righteous— persons of integrity—as those who meditate with "two books," the book of nature and the book of scriptures, secular and sacred as one.

> Happy are those whose ... delight is in the Torah of the Lord,
> and on God's law they meditate day and night.
> They are like trees planted by streams of water,
> which yield their fruit in its season.
> Psalm 1:2–3, AT

The 150 Psalms follow the template of the first one, yearning for the divine presence in all life's seasons: in suffering and success, pain and potential, perishing and prospering.

For cultivating honest to God awareness, the Psalms provide "an anatomy of all parts of the soul," to borrow Protestant reformer John

Calvin's metaphor. They echo all the soul's moods: exhilaration and exhaustion, anger and apathy, divine presence and absence. In the same breath, these prayers equally question *and* celebrate God's love:

> Will the Lord spurn forever, and never again be favorable?
> Has God forgotten to be gracious?
>   Psalm 77: 7–9

Then after the person praying ponders and meditates to recall past experiences of divine presence (77:10–12), the mood shifts.

> Your way, O God, is holy.
> What God is so great as our God?
>   Psalm 77:13

I call this the "spirituality of the fishhook." You pray down into the anguish with soul-searching questions, recollect past experiences, and only then does your mood swing up with affirmation to catch a glimpse of hope. Yet the affirmation may end with another question.

But what about anger and rage in the Psalms? I've found a helpful insight based on psychiatrist Carl Jung: What I don't like in the Psalms often reflects part of myself that I don't like. For example, I cringe when the Psalms express raw hatred and violence: "I hate them with perfect hatred" (139:22). So by praying the raw, uncensored stuff, I notice and offer parts of myself I often suppress.

> As the tree of life shows us, prayer is a way of being rooted and grounded in love.

These ancient psalm prayers express raw emotions of the soul and invite you and me to create our own psalm prayers that counterpoint the gore and glory in the "what is" of life, beginning by listening to our own self-talk.

Psalm writers interweave God-talk with their self-talk—then listen for whispers of sacred response. Today people commonly use "self" for "soul" (*nefesh* in Hebrew), so I'm going to use that substitution to make the point that talking to your self is surely a form of psalm-like praying, as in these examples of sadness and joy.

Why are you cast down, O my self,
and why are you disquieted within me?
    Psalm 42:5, AT

Bless the Lord, O my self, and all that is within me,
bless God's holy name.
    Psalm 103:1, AT

Ask yourself again, what's really important for me? Then ask, what gets in the way of my attentiveness to that? Try writing your own psalm. Sitting in Chicago's O'Hare International Airport, I began conversing with my listless self as I heard the droning TSA announcement.

Unattended Baggage

Attention all passengers:
Do not leave baggage unattended.
Any unattended baggage will be
confiscated and may be destroyed.

Unattended baggage is the silent
witness you inherit from sleeping
generations, accumulated stuff
from infant's primal scream
to adolescent's ingenious schemes
to adulthood's stifled dreams.

Your unattended baggage sits
locked in guarded rooms,

unclaimed treasures stacked
in corners, dark upon dark,
each one growing heavier,
mustier by the decade,
awaiting lost identities.

Any unattended baggage
will be confiscated by agents
of your neglect's own choosing.

Yet the very moment you attend
to any neglected items, you befriend
forgotten parts of your self, waiting
to say, *Thank you. I've been wanting
to come home to your heart. Welcome.*

It occurred to me that parts of our selves we've forgotten—even from our ancestors—may contain our souls' treasures. The Hindu Chandogya Upanishad (8.3.2) says, "One not knowing that a golden treasure lies buried beneath his feet may walk over it again and again, yet never find it."

Mostly we start out interested in the treasure for what's in it for ourselves: prayer may begin by loving the self for the self's sake—to get out of trouble or stay out of trouble.

But just realizing there *is* a treasure cracks the door to a deeper desire. In his poem "A Man Talking to His House," the Muslim Sufi poet Rumi says that life is like a caravan where no one is awake and "that while you sleep, a thief is stealing" the things you think are your life. "Pay attention," he says, because someone who hurts your feelings may be telling you the truth.[4]

How can you learn to live awake, so that the thief of your own boredom—or numbing yourself to life's pain—doesn't rob you of your treasure? Honest to God prayer means digging through the rubble to find the treasure beneath your feet.

CHAPTER TWO

Living Awake
to What Is

The Process of Awareness

I don't like work—no man does—but I like what is in the
work, the chance to find yourself. Your own reality.
—JOSEPH CONRAD, *HEART OF DARKNESS*

Days pass, years vanish, and we walk sightless among miracles.
—HEBREW PRAYER

*L*iving awake means cultivating awareness: being with what is changes what
was and what will be. What would such a process look like? The only
reality you have is in the lens you use to see it. People can create their
own reality with a self-defeating script from childhood or tragic circumstances. "Whether you think you can or can't, you're right," the saying
goes. So if you change the lens on that reality, the story you tell yourself,
then the situation actually changes for you. You awaken to a new Reality.

When you hear people say, "It is what it is," the expression
sounds fatalistic, resigned. But "being with what is changes what was
and what will be"—this calls you to see something more.

The process of being with what is means work. Sometimes through outer work, sometimes through inner work, you discover a glimpse of a greater work—a taste of passion for why you're here on this earth. In spiritual terms, the work becomes grace. That's when you can say with Joseph Conrad, "I like what is in the work, the chance to find yourself. Your own reality." Grace is divine acceptance of who I am in my own real world.

Edwin Friedman, who wrote *Generation to Generation*, is often cited for making into a household phrase the idea that you can be a "non-anxious presence." Being an anxious type of personality myself, I was eager to converse with Friedman about a holistic weaving of psychology and spirituality. I knew Friedman was not advocating stoic spirituality that would deny the need to be real with your own angst. Out of the synergy of our conversation, this is what emerged in my awareness: Being a non-anxious presence does not mean having no anxiety; rather, it means being so present to your anxiety that it becomes a creative source of connection with your true self, with God, with others, and with the universe.

> Being with what is changes what was and what will be.

Being with what is changes what was and what will be: that statement requires no God-talk or God concepts. It can be a good place to start if part of you thinks of yourself as "spiritual but not religious." What would it mean to "be with" what's going on in your world—so that you don't walk sightless among miracles?

Soul-Searching Questions: Deepening What Is

Honest to God prayer beckons you to notice what is, to offer those stirrings, and to listen. You get in touch with your own soul-searching questions and engage in psalm-like praying. That can even mean questioning the whole idea of God.

Who Is the You I Pray To?

Who is the *you* I pray to?
Is it some extraterrestrial being
I'm addressing when I say "Lord"?
Is it some mega-size he or she,
some humanized projection
of my personal wants, god in my image,
the future of my own illusion?
Is this *you* some amalgam of our national
fantasies to protect a lifestyle
impossible for the rest of the planet?
Whatever "it" is, this god has to die,
or has already died.

What if the *you* I pray to
is my higher self—the Christ self,
the ideal human hope for a Love Supreme
that can only take shape in the web
of interconnectedness with all my relations,
my human siblings and rocks, rivers,
mountains, deserts, glaciers?

What if the *you* I pray to
is at once you and us and me and we,
the yearning to be free to love? What if such
a web is the all-surrounding string-theory
universe that stretches out and in
and through—within all things,
the primal Love Force in whom we live
and move and have our being?
What if the *you* I pray to
became one of us?

Soul-searching, psalm-like questions create fertile compost for being with what is, to begin a deeper spiritual journey, or begin again. You practice the theology of the fishhook, diving into a struggle until you find an upswing of insight. You can practice the art of creative questions by writing in a journal, by silently meditating with a Zen-like question—or by conversing with a trained spiritual guide.

As I practice the ancient art of spiritual companioning, when a person presents me with an impossible catch-22, instead of giving an answer, often I pause to convert my insight into a question. That creates another pause. Amazingly, the insight emerges from the person. Once, when a friend felt stymied by his own lethargy, I asked, what did he think God might want to say? After a silence, he said, "I think God may be saying, *Try to remember what you already know.*" I asked, what did he already know? Insights poured out.

Two other ancient ideas can rekindle the soul through awareness: to restore the honesty, curiosity, and playfulness of the child within and to practice multiple levels of Socrates' ancient wisdom, "Know thyself."

Whole-Self Prayer: Restoring the Playful Child

To restore the healthy child in yourself is to live with soul, awake with all the senses to life's pain and play. Returning to a childlike habit of mind lies at the heart of nearly every spiritual tradition.

In Native traditions, facing east at sunrise symbolizes renewing the child within. "The great person is one who does not lose the child's heart," writes Confucian leader Mencius in the third century BCE. When Jesus tells a Jewish teacher, Nicodemus, that "to see the kingdom of God" he must be born anew, he takes Jesus literally: "Can one enter a second time into the mother's womb and be born?" (John 3:3). The Sufi Muslim poet Hafiz asks God to "take care of that / Holy infant my heart has become."[1]

Creative breakthroughs wed the most advanced theories of science or politics or theology with the innocent wonder of a child. It's what I call playful projects for serious purposes. Margaret Geller, chief scientist at the Smithsonian Astrological Observatory, says, "The best scientists are those who retain the somewhat naïve curiosity of a child. They see the world with a special eye."

Isn't that the goal of prayer: to see the world with a special eye? We cannot *do* the restoring; we can only train the eye of awareness to see the bush when it blazes.

Soul (*nefesh*) inhabits the whole person in Jewish spirituality: "Bless the Lord, O my soul, and *all* that is within me, bless God's holy name" (Psalm 103:1, AT). The *Shema,* as we noted, bids us listen, to love God with all our soul, which includes heart, mind, and body—your whole being (Deuteronomy 6:4; Mark 12:29). To restore the soul is to renew the healthy child within the elder, both archetypes in each of us. I call this *whole-self prayer.*

> Isn't that the goal of prayer: to see the world with a special eye?

Yet *soul* sounds so diffuse, non-quantifiable. What practical ways can restore the soul in our active working, parenting, communicating, and recreating? Honest to God prayer integrates the child and the elder, heart and mind, spontaneity and seriousness.

Living Awake to the Whole Self: Multiple Intelligences and Soul

The multiple intelligences approach to learning, pioneered and developed by Harvard educator Howard Gardner over three decades, offers practical, creative frames for noticing, offering, and listening in all of life.[2] Particular modes of learning are highly developed in a person, in others less, yet everyone has some aptitude in each. I aim to show how these nine frames of mind, as Gardner calls them, can reframe any profane or profound experience as an occasion for prayer and spiritual awakening.

Here I offer a playful, prayerful perspective on these nine ways of tending the soul's gifts and struggles, always with an eye to a sense of invitation.

1. *Linguistic/verbal*: Prayer articulates the soul's yearnings by playing with words in sacred texts with stories and poetry. As a child can't survive in isolation, so a spiritual seeker needs relationships to listen and learn the language of love.
2. *Logical/mathematical*: Techno*logical* tools connect kindred spirits via the Internet; theo*logical* ideas make sense of crazy experiences. The Bible and Jewish kabbalistic spirituality play with sacred numbers, like seven, to signify wholeness.
3. *Spatial/visual*: Our souls resound with awe in temples and cathedrals, with intimacy in house churches. We play and pray by exploring geography, cultural exchanges, holy places, labyrinths—and inner spaces of imagination (like Narnia).
4. *Musical/rhythmic*: "One who sings prays twice," said Augustine. Drums, chants, strings, and poetry's beat echo the soul's sorrow and joys; jazz makes the blues beautiful; African American spirituals unite personal and political struggles.
5. *Kinesthetic/bodily*: The Spirit inhabits our breathing from our borning cry to our wordless sighs; gestures, used to direct players in a symphony or a ball game, can express the soul's prayers in bowing, kneeling, dancing, or walking a labyrinth.
6. *Interpersonal*: Extroverts tend to encounter the Sacred in community, introverts in small groups or one-on-one; both experience the Holy in playful and genuine relationships, as a surprise line of a conversation can be a prayer or an epiphany.
7. *Intrapersonal*: Prayerful contemplation and playful reflection thrive in solitude, which is sorely neglected in our technological society; silence nurtures an introvert's joy and preserves an extrovert's sanity; journaling dream associations unlocks prayers.

8. *Naturalist*: Our primal yearnings resonate with natural environments, playfully and prayerfully responding to the Sacred in awe and beauty, in patterns of devastation and renewal in nature, human nature, and nations.

9. *Existentialist*: Honest to God prayer can play and pray with the "why" questions of an Einstein, a three-year-old, or a philosopher: Why are we here? What's it all about? How shall we then live?

These nine perspectives integrate our primal knowing with our modern knowledge for a genuine holistic approach to prayer. For nearly four centuries, René Descartes's maxim "I think, therefore I am" skewed modern Western culture toward logical and technological intelligence. But if you examine only what you "think" about God, you can end up feeling like a spiritual flunky. Actually you may "know" the Holy in your experience, your gut, your heart—your primal brain. Today's spiritual quest is to link our primal yearnings with our modern learnings, and these nine frames of mind act as links in a transformative chain reaction.

Some ask, where are the spiritual and emotional intelligences? I was with Gardner for a weeklong seminar when he was still deciding what to name the ninth intelligence. During a break, I said, "I hope you never call it a spiritual or religious intelligence." Why would I say that when I'm a minister and spiritual writer? Because, he affirmed, spiritual and emotional dimensions are woven throughout all nine, and to create a separate category would split the soul from the essence of life.

The ancient Greek Archimedes sprang naked out of his bath when a new scientific truth struck him, shouting, *Eureka! Eureka!*—"I've found it! I've found it!" Singer-songwriter John Denver sang about nature's "Rocky Mountain High." French mathematician and philosopher Blaise Pascal encountered the mystic Christ via his mathematical calculations. Brother Lawrence was converted by seeing a barren tree in winter. Psalms are full of naturalist wonders and kinesthetic spiritual gestures: walking, climbing, bowing, kneeling, clapping, and lifting hands. And the existentialist questions of your life create the seedbed for the Spirit. Prayer embodies spirituality in every sphere of life—emotional, mental, and physical.

Creative stories also participate in facets of all nine modes: witness stories told as operas, musicals, ballads, dances, and dramas. A Hasidic story tells of a *rebbe*, a respected Jewish teacher, who was crippled and bedfast for years. In struggling to light the first Hanukkah candle, he began to tell how his grandfather used to sing and dance. As the old man was telling it he hobbled on his twisted feet and began singing and dancing.[3]

> As a fruit of prayer, we begin to see that self-growth can be God-growth— a deeper Self beyond the self we know.

These nine lenses create a practical, observable template to renew holistic spirituality in language, reason, imagination, body, music, relationships, solitude, nature, and questions.

We can get too comfortable with the often-quoted wisdom, "Pray as you can, and not as you can't." Consider an addendum to stretch the soul: "Until I try some ways I think I can't pray, I don't know quite so well how I can" (see Prayer Practice 3). You might get to know yourself in surprising new ways.

Knowing Self, Knowing God

Knowing self and knowing God are double threads interweaving in a spiritual tapestry. "The more conception of God, the more self; the more self, the more conception of God," wrote Søren Kierkegaard. As a fruit of prayer, we begin to see that self-growth can be God-growth— a deeper Self beyond the self we know. Prayer is a way of getting to know yourself as well as God knows you.

O Lord, you have searched me and known me.

You know when I sit down and when I rise up;

you discern my thoughts from far away.

> Psalm 139:1–2

But how can we live fully into this process of divine-human awareness in life's grit? Is such attentiveness really prayer?

"Attention is the only faculty of the soul that gives us access to God." These words of the French Christian mystic and political activist Simone Weil were engraved after her death on a postage stamp issued by the French government in her honor. I could also say that attention—living awake to what is—is the only faculty of the soul that gives us access to the gifts within our own self. Socrates said, "Know yourself." But how?

"Experience is the best teacher," people say. But as friends in Alcoholics Anonymous are quick to tell me, you can cycle through the same experience over and over, and never really learn from it. So I've begun to say, "Experience reflected upon is the real teacher."

Again, Socrates says, "The unexamined life is not worth living." And if that's true, we need a corollary: "The examined life is worth living twice." That's what the classic practice of examen is all about—harvesting the fruits of lived experience.

As described by Ignatius of Loyola in *The Spiritual Exercises*, examen is a method of prayerful reflection on the events of the day in order to discern God's presence and direction for us. You use all the senses, becoming aware of the day's experiences and emotions related to those events.

First, you pause to notice *gifts* in a given day, cultivating gratitude and a sense of divine presence. Second, you notice places of *struggle*, acknowledging areas of tension in your daily journey. Third, in light of what's going on, you ask, what's the *invitation*—how is Life or God inviting me to move forward in the day ahead? In Ignatius's thought, you ask, what grace—what spiritual blessing—do I need to pray for to be more whole?

Examen is a way of being with what is and seeing it change (see Prayer Practice 2). Following are examples of integrating the multiple intelligences with the process of examen to live fully awake.

NOTICING ENVIRONMENTS

In *Dakota: A Spiritual Geography*, Kathleen Norris tells of her early years working for the North Dakota Arts Council, being sequestered for weeks in motels with a rusty tin shower and a pay phone in the parking lot. Then she began to apply her learning from the fourth-century desert monks: "I began to see those forlorn motel rooms as monks' cells, full of the gifts of silence and solitude." It amused the Arts Council staff, but it worked for her. "I found that I could knit, work on my writing, and do serious reading; in short, be in the desert and let it bloom."[4] Examen means noticing and offering what is, then listening for an invitation in it.

NOTICING THE BODY

The body takes the shape of the soul. If you think about it, the opposite is also true: *The soul takes the shape of the body.* If the body is tense, as Herbert Benson demonstrated in his popular book *The Relaxation Response*, our physical, spiritual, and emotional health is at risk. The spiritual journey can begin, or begin again, by finding the gift in the grit of the body's aches and ecstasies, its abilities and disabilities. There is no such thing as disembodied spirituality (see Prayer Practice 5).

The body can bring us home through the joy of life-giving sexuality: we sweat, we groan, we know beyond words. Our bodies hold the golden key to savor ecstatic moments and to release painful stress, directing each into spiritual and vocational energy.

After surgery for a back injury in 1974, I literally "backed" into disciplined practices of meditation and prayer. Prescribed exercises have become gestures of gratitude or prayers for others. I've found ways to incorporate liturgical prayers, scriptures, and breathing meditations. I still go through times of intense pain. Writing creates another way to redirect the body's pain. Recently, while teaching a writing class at Chautauqua, New York, my wife had to carry my backpack. I wrote in my journal:

Painting Pain

Is there beneath
this pain some gain
that I might miss
if I complain?
Is there within
my complaint some
vibrant pigment
I can use to paint
suffering's landscape,
to reinvent my pain
into a space for all
humanity to trace
an arc of beauty in
the dust and rain?

NOTICING EMOTIONS

Meditative writing, art, music, yoga, or tai chi—any of these can create a container for processing emotions to find an invitation in your angst or bliss. Once a student mentioned that envy might signal a person's vocational passion. It got me pondering: I'm not envious at all when I hear of a sports hero who makes it big, but let me hear of a spiritual writer or poet with a fantastic bestseller—now that touches my passion! To notice, offer, and listen to any raw emotion of the soul can convert negative energy into healing.

NOTICING NATURE

I recall a transformative moment from my Penn State days, while attending an InterVarsity Christian Fellowship leadership retreat at Cedar Campus on Michigan's Upper Peninsula. One evening's speaker said something like, "This afternoon I noticed several of you talking about spiritual things, while seemingly oblivious to nature's incredible beauty all about you." Had we been oblivious to the crystalline lake, the cobalt sky, butternut saplings, ancient tamaracks, gigantic birch, amazing flora and fauna? I took away a message: if you want to relate spirituality to people, you need to pay attention to the world around you. You can practice with an open-eyed table blessing (see Prayer Practice 6).

NOTICING PEOPLE

Training the eyes of the heart links awareness and action. My friend Bobbie got involved in MADD (Mothers *and others* Against Drunk Driving, as she likes to say), after recovering from critical injuries in a car crash. One evening a State Police officer presented the state MADD board with a group police photo for use in MADD advertising. Ordinarily a quiet person, Bobbie spoke out, "I don't see any women or people of color in this photograph." The police officials did a retake of the photo. Sheer noticing became a small act of justice.

NOTICING YOUR STORIES

Stories have power to shape our lives. The mark of a life-giving story often involves a downturn into an impasse followed by an upturn into some fruit born of the struggle. Try connecting your stories to the arc of stories in scriptures of your own faith tradition (see chapter four).

NOTICING YOUR DREAMING

Dreams signal your soul to wake up. Paying attention to night dreams and also to luminous daytime moments can direct your life's passion and purpose. And that's the next step in waking up, to claim your possibilities and live your dreams (see chapter four).

Practicing for Surprise

Many folks are praying merely by being with what is, in expectation of something holy, or wholly by surprise. Such moments in the process of awakening occur on the road far more often than in a temple or during personal prayer. So why bother with corporate disciplines or personal prayer practices? Anthony de Mello's thoughts, adapted from *One Minute Wisdom*, prod us.

> *Disciples to Master*: How difficult is enlightenment?
>
> *Master*: Oh, it is effortless, like the sunrise!
>
> *Disciples*: Then why all these difficult practices?
>
> *Master*: Ah! So that you will be awake when the sun rises.

Practices for Cultivating Awareness

Beginning Prayer If You Can't Pray

People talk about not being able to pray. Religious language may get in the way. Try substituting the word *yearn* for *pray*. What is it you really yearn for, beneath the things and experiences you spend so much time on? To paraphrase several ancient mystics, merely the desire to pray is already prayer. You wouldn't be thinking about prayer if you didn't want to pray. Spend twenty minutes listening to your desire, your longing, your yearning. Consider how that may be your prayer. Reflect inwardly or make a few notes in your journal.

Prayer Practice 2

A Daily Prayer of Reflection and Examen

Imagine you invite the Sacred Light of the world to walk with you, scanning over the past twenty-four hours (or recent period). Breathe deeply: in … out…. Gently sift through events and encounters…. Imagine scenes unfolding as from a slow-moving train.

1. Gift (Wow!) *As you reflect on your day, notice and give thanks for specific gift(s).* Celebrate God's empowering love at a time or times when you felt loved or loving.
2. Struggle (Whoa.) *Notice times when you struggled to feel loved or loving.* Observe any unrest or unresolved tension in your soul. Celebrate God's undefeated love and hear: "You are my beloved."
3. Invitation (What now?) *Ask: What grace do I need to name and claim to be more whole today?* Allow a word or phrase— an image or metaphor—to come to mind. Begin to repeat it, slowly with your breathing, or picture it if it's an image (silence).

Personal option: Try imagining a mini-hidden video at home or work, visualizing yourself acting as if you are already whole.

Group option: Share with one other person (four or five minutes). Conclude with a brief silent prayer for each other. Then invite the whole group to reflect on the experience.

Prayer Practice 3

Expanding Personal Prayer

Glance over the nine multiple intelligences. Now review your personal spiritual practices. Notice one or two of the nine modes that are least present in your prayer life. Challenge yourself to choose a couple that stretch your normal pattern. For example, if most of your prayers are verbal, you might ask how you might develop intrapersonal practices (silence, centering prayer) or kinesthetic practices (gestures such as kneeling, stretching, dancing; tensing and releasing hands).

Group option: Invite group members to share one-on-one, then as a whole group.

Prayer Practice 4

Centering Prayer as Contemplative Practice

Meditate on your real desire or yearning beneath all the doing of ministry. Allow a simple word to arise, one that seems to sum up that deep longing. Examples: *Love, Peace, Trust*; or a short phrase of scripture such as "Be still, and know...." (Psalm 46:10)—or just "Be...." For some persons, a word in another language helps avoid thinking: *Amor* ("love"); *Shalom* ("peace" in Hebrew) or *Salaam* ("peace" in Arabic); *Maranatha* ("Our Lord come" in Aramaic). Or a visual image or metaphor may arise. Begin repeating it, gently, in rhythm to your breathing.... Or visualizing it.... Then let go of the word or image: simply allow yourself to be present, loving and being loved. Aim to cultivate twenty minutes of contemplative silence daily (or at least four days out of seven); log reflections in your journal.

Option: Set a timer or smartphone so you are free from concern for time; promise yourself at least two minutes if you can't take twenty.

Prayer Practice 5

Meditative Thanks with Your Body

Sit in silence, and slow down your breathing. Allow a centering word or phrase to arise (like "Here I am," or *hineini* in Hebrew), or a quieting image, such as a babbling brook. Repeat it slowly if it's a word, or visualize it if it's an image. In many spiritual streams, the body is the temple of the Spirit, and genuine worship begins by presenting one's body. Inhale lovingly … meditate … exhale thankfully…. Begin inhaling while tensing your left foot, then release it when exhaling … right foot … left ankle … each area of the body up through your abdomen … to your heart … then each shoulder, arm, hand … return to your larynx … parts of the face … to the top of your head…. Gratefully bask in an aura of peace. When you finish, use your journal to write reflections from the experience.

Option: Using your journal, doodle a pencil sketch of your body, noting areas that need attention.

Prayer Practice 6

Open-Eyed Table Blessing

This table grace can be used at home or at a community gathering. The leader says: "Be aware of our unity with all people and creation … breathing in the same air with rich and poor. Notice the food … smells … colors…. Imagine the seeds … the dark soil … the bright sun … farmers planting it … migrant farm laborers harvesting it with their hands … people transporting and preparing it with their hands. Gently lift your hands on behalf of all who work with their hands." Conclude by saying in Spanish, *¡Gracias!* (meaning both thanks, and grace for those in need) three times in unison, *¡Gracias! ¡Gracias! ¡Gracias!*

Prayer as Empowerment

Expanding

CHAPTER THREE

Claiming Possibilities

The Grounding for Empowerment

To pray is to breathe, and possibility is for the self what
oxygen is for breathing. But for possibility alone or for
necessity alone to supply the conditions for the breathing
of prayer is no more possible than it is for a [person] to
breathe oxygen alone or nitrogen alone.
        —SØREN KIERKEGAARD, SICKNESS UNTO DEATH

May God grant you your heart's desire, and fulfill all
your plans.
        —PSALM 20:4

*T*he next step after waking up is to begin claiming your gifts. Prayer as reality means noticing and offering to God what is, and that includes
your half-denied regrets for what might have been as well as your
half-repressed fantasies of what can still be—which leads us to prayer
as possibility. This is the noon of life and its direction is the South,
expanding upward like the sun, where in primal traditions you claim

your powers of generativity and vocation—your purpose and passion for living, fruitfulness that extends beyond career or job.

Now that you're aware that a "golden treasure lies buried beneath [your] feet," it's time to claim it, as a Hindu Upanishad invites. For Jesus, the treasure is the kingdom of heaven: while it's within me, it's not just mine but for the good of the whole realm. Spiritual empowerment is your unique "treasure hidden in a field," your unique "pearl of great value," and to realize it may mean sacrificing everything else (Matthew 13:44–45). This is prayer that moves mountains and says, with God nothing is impossible.

On a human level, you may have experienced being in a crowd and sensing that someone was staring at you. A simple experiment can validate the power of focused energy (see Prayer Practice 7).

> Spiritual empowerment is your unique "treasure hidden in a field," your unique "pearl of great value," and to realize it may mean sacrificing everything else (Matthew 13:44–45).

Prayer is a means of tapping your human energies for creative spiritual purposes.

Kierkegaard compares prayer to breathing in as possibility (expanding) and breathing out as necessity (emptying), movements essential to healthy spirituality (see Prayer Practice 8). How can you breathe in possibility to connect your inner dreams with outer reality?

The grounding for empowerment theme explores *qualities* of authentic spiritual energies. Then, in the next chapter, the process of empowerment will explore *methods* for connecting those energies to the world's needs.

This grounding itself is a form of prayer. Creative Christian author C. S. Lewis describes prayer as "unveiling," making known to oneself and God what is really in our minds and hearts. In *Letters to Malcolm: Chiefly on Prayer*, Lewis says, "It is no use to ask God with factitious earnestness for **A** when our whole mind is in reality filled with the desire for **B**. We must lay before [God] what is in us, not what ought to be in us."[1] Genuine empowering prayer begins with what is and moves to what can be.

Struggles between Spirituality and Power

Honest to God prayer frees and empowers the human spirit to love. So why do many find it hard to speak of spirituality as empowerment? Is it that people equate raw power with money and status, the world's way of doing things? Is it because power doesn't seem to square with the humility factor that's so integral to authentic spirituality? Because Jesus and the Buddha leave behind royal power and family for the sake of the calling to be mystical teachers, how do you reconcile self-denial with self-empowerment?

Or is it that power gets identified with coercive religion, with systems and leaders that have perpetrated crusades and a crusade mentality, and the oppression of women and native peoples? Today you can point to religious extremism that fuels violence, even among various religions. (You can equally make the case that spirituality, and even religion, has been a powerful force for justice. Witness the nineteenth-century abolitionist movement in the United States and the twentieth-century civil rights movement.)

Then there's the feel-good "health and wealth" type of commercial spirituality, where power seems mostly about ego. Whether TV evangelists marketing a prosperity gospel (just have faith) or the more sophisticated movie *What the Bleep Do We Know!?* and New Thought guru Rhonda Byrne's popular book *The Secret* (just focus), each message seems to say you have the power to create your reality for health and wealth. To each I might ask: What if you're not healed or don't get rich? Is something wrong with your *faith*—or your *focus*?

What if you ask deeper questions: What would it look like to name and claim your gifts in times of success *and* suffering? What do you plan to use your gifts *for*?

Honest to God Empowerment

Honest to God empowerment means noticing, offering, and listening to your gifts in order to claim your own potential for transforming the world.

Marilyn had come for spiritual guidance. Once she got settled, I asked, "What would be the prayer of your heart as we converse today?" After pausing while I lighted a candle, she said, "For grounding." A question, with a pause, had empowered her to draw on guidance from within herself.

Grounding was ideal for her situation, as she began saying she was considering an inner sense of call to a big change related to her vocation. Noticing some discomfort with certain policies in her present social service work, Marilyn had begun exploring the possibility of founding a new center in a neighborhood where there were no such services. As she offered some of her dreams and fantasies of what might be, she began to listen to new dimensions, challenges, possibilities, and connections stirring within her. To notice, offer, and listen—alone or in community—creates the grounding for honest to God empowerment.

Qualities for Empowering the Best Self

This grounding begins by noticing inner and outer nudgings, hints of what Quakers call "way" closing behind you—or "way" opening before you. Empowerment is all about discerning your vocation: to offer hints of your passion means to experiment with your nudgings, to test your leadings. Prayer not only keeps your eyes awake to possibilities; prayer also cultivates the essential qualities for claiming your gifts.

As you cultivate inner qualities of passion, compassion, gratitude, imagination, and openness to surprise, they build on each other as your inner work and your outer work connect with glimpses of the greater work.

PASSION

Living awake to your passion is the most important quality in claiming your gifts. Offering your inner vocational nudgings expands honest to God prayer, which started with inklings of awareness. These hints may simply nudge you to attend to your present tasks with rekindled passion or they may call you to a nobler cause. It's a personal laboratory experiment to find out what kindles your deepest spiritual energies.

Far from stifling your passion, you are invited to voice it: "May God grant you your heart's desire, and fulfill all your plans" (Psalm 20:4). Your prayers begin to give voice to your hunches.

I've noticed at least three things come to mind when people talk about passion: *energy*, *suffering*, and *sexuality*. First, passion embodies deep heart and gut energy—expressed in violent rage or in ecstatic delight. Energy is neutral, and can be used for evil or for good: Hitler used his passion to destroy humanity; Mother Teresa used her passion to ennoble humanity. Genuine prayer as empowerment transforms destructive anger into a passionate cause for mending the universe, as Mahatma Gandhi or Nelson Mandela demonstrate.

> To notice, offer, and listen—alone or in community—creates the grounding for honest to God empowerment.

Second, passion involves suffering. Your inner energies, born out of your own woundedness and giftedness, connect with some outward suffering in the world. The word *passion* is based on the Latin *passum*, from *patior* (the root of patience), meaning "to suffer, undergo, or experience." As European psychologist Alice Miller shows in her classic *The Drama of the Gifted Child*, many people who are passionate about a cause have experienced some abuse or suffering that lies at the root of their transformed passion.

Third, passion is deeply rooted in our sexuality, as folks speak of passionate lovers. Sexuality can be the source of our deepest pain and bliss. I mean sexuality in its deeper and broader sense, beyond the joy of physical sex. You are ultimately fulfilled as your sexuality draws you to bearing fruit in the world in a unique way. In chapter four, I will show how sexuality serves as a key element in discerning your vocation. Living awake to your passion empowers you to bear the fruit of compassion.

COMPASSION

How do these qualities of passion become prayer? How can I live awake with my energy, suffering, and sexuality? Prayer means "being with" your passion (*com* + *passion*). Compassion is love with skin on. After Jesus says to love God with your whole being comes the part saying to love your neighbor as yourself, quoting the Hebrew Bible. I view these as a three-way cyclical interaction: sometimes having compassion for your own self—your gifts and wounds—keeps you awake to God; other times having compassion for a suffering neighbor keeps you awake to your true self; sometimes a mystical brush with God's compassion keeps you living awake to self and neighbor.

Compassion is the bedrock quality of genuine spiritual empowerment in every major spiritual tradition: the Golden Rule in its many variants. Rabbi Hillel was once asked if he could recite the entire Torah in the time he could stand on one foot. He replied, "What is hateful to you, do not do unto others. This is the whole Torah." Jesus turned the phrase: "Do to others as you would have them do to you; for this is the law and the prophets" (Matthew 7:12). Confucius and the Buddha express the same golden ethic of reciprocity. To adapt a line from Atticus to his daughter, Scout, in Harper Lee's classic *To Kill a Mockingbird*, "You never really understand a person until you consider things from his or her point of view, until you climb inside their skin and walk around in it."

So the Golden Rule begins with an act of contemplating: Wait a minute, not just what would *I* want—but what would I want done to me if I were in *their* shoes? Every good action arises out of contemplation. Through prayer, you step out of the container of your experience into someone else's, and your passion morphs into compassion.

GRATITUDE

A student meeting with me was recounting moments of gratitude when he paused and said, "The heart of gratitude is the rich soil that virtues grow out of." Immediately I thought how in Elizabethan English "virtue" can mean "power."

The prayer practice of examen acts as a magnet to notice gratitude in everyday observations, what poet Jane Kenyon called the "luminous particular," where you lose yourself in awareness. With examen, you scan over your day, notice and give thanks for some gift(s). You celebrate God's empowering love at a time or times when you felt loved or loving (see Prayer Practice 2).

You know it's prayer when keen awareness of the ordinary leads you to that point where the ego self dies and you awaken to your best self—which for me I call the Christ self. By practicing the art of recall-

> Compassion is the bedrock quality of genuine spiritual empowerment in every major spiritual tradition: the Golden Rule in its many variants.

ing gifts and struggles each day and looking for an invitation to grow through each layer of experience, you are empowering yourself with gratitude, building on your strengths. The final point of the examen is to imagine yourself acting as if you were already whole. In such a moment of holy imagination, you are empowered.

Gratitude can also empower community. Appreciative Inquiry (AI) functions as a kind of communal version of examen. AI, developed by organizational behavior pioneer David Cooperrider, is a planning process that gathers the community's gifts and stories, always with an intention to build on their strengths. In such ways the practice of gratitude builds confidence and fuels personal and communal vision and imagination.

IMAGINATION

"It is at the level of imagination that the fateful issues of our new world-experience must first be mastered," says the early twentieth-century poet-theologian Amos Wilder. Visualizing yourself as complete can be a method of focusing and a form of prayer (see Prayer Practice 2). Imagination also creates a powerful way to pray without words for another: You visualize the person in your mind's eye as already whole and complete, holding the person in the light—a practice called kything prayer (see Prayer Practice 9).

Imagination can also transform struggles into gifts. Philip Schultz, a Pulitzer Prize–winning poet and author of the memoir *My Dyslexia*, tells his story of being placed in the "dummy class" at a separate table in elementary school because of his perceived stupidity for not being able to read.

Then one night, with the moon glowing outside his window as his mother read aloud to him, he decided to imagine himself into being a boy who could read: "I invented a character who could read and write. Starting that night, I'd lie in bed silently imitating the words my mother read, imagining the taste, heft, and ring of each sound as if it were coming out of my mouth. I imagined the words and their sounds being a kind of key with which I would open an invisible door to a world previously denied me."[2]

"To this day," Schulz says, "I can't attend a High Holy Day service at my synagogue without feeling I don't belong there, because I can't speak Hebrew and must pretend to read my prayer book." For me, that is honest to God prayer: his not praying verbally is a deeper prayer; it's praying with the heart. Sometimes merely the desire to pray is already prayer (see Prayer Practice 1).

Ignatius of Loyola is known for his highly developed use of the imagination. In *The Spiritual Exercises*, Ignatius invites you to imagine yourself in the scenes of scriptures, to visualize yourself as the beggar or as the paralyzed person now coming alive—or as the poor woman touching Jesus's garment, immune to others' criticism while receiving the full attention of the Lord of love. So imagination is integrated with real-life situations.

YOUR OWN VOICE

Expressing your passion as compassion means finding your voice, or letting your voice find you: that is genuine empowerment. "If you ask me what I have come to do in the world, I will tell you: I am here to live out loud," says French novelist Emile Zola. Offering your voice can take you outside the box of religion. To claim your voice means to live out and to pray from your unique personality, cultural heritage, and sexual orientation. Spiritually, claiming your voice embodies the whole person, as when Gandhi says, "My life is my message."

Empowerment is the passionate *must* to express your own voice; for some it emerges like a gentle horse whisperer while for others it explodes like a volcano. Three resources can help you to express your unique voice. First, the *lectio* method of praying with scripture and in all of life is adaptable for all personality types (see Prayer Practice 10). Second, the multiple intelligences offer a framework to give voice to your passion and claim your gifts in every aspect of life (see chapter two). Third, the discernment process from *The Spiritual Exercises* of Ignatius of Loyola integrates both cognitive and affective processes, internal and external data, spiritual and factual experiences (see "Choosing Well, Living Whole" at the end of chapter four).

SILENCE AND SOLITUDE

The practice of silence—claiming soul space—can tap a vast reservoir of unconscious potential for authentic prayer. Pauses for silence during the day, as Alcoholics Anonymous recommends, create what I call "Your Portable Monastery" (see Prayer Practice 11). Scheduling an occasional period of retreat for personal prayer and reflection allows you to listen to books and sermons already written in your heart. A college professor thanked me for suggesting that he leave his books and e-reader at home and take nothing but his Bible and a journal to a monastery.

Claiming soul space can empower relationships. Shawna told of traveling out of state to spend holidays with her family. A sister expected her to be available 24/7. But Shawna found herself telling her sister, "I need to take some time for quiet, and then I'll be more attentive and present with you." It worked, she said, and her sister seemed to relish the deeper conversations and the rhythm of alone times. Honest prayer has everything to do with claiming space for your soul to breathe amid the tensions of family- or work-related constrictions, which, if unattended over time, can suffocate your soul. Breaking a codependent pattern on a small scale can act as a mini-paradigm for changing big obstacles that set you up for spiritual and emotional burnout.

SURPRISE

The purpose of spiritual practices is to keep the soul aware and open to surprise epiphanies on a personal level, and on an organizational level as well.

An eleven-year-old boy was watching an evening news clip that showed a homeless man sleeping on the street in downtown Philadelphia on a bitterly cold night. Trevor Farrell insisted his parents drive him from their suburban Gladwyne home to the city that night. Ignoring his mother's plea merely to open the car window, he darted from the car to hand the man his own blanket and pillow. A single TV news clip had spread its roots in Trevor, until eventually his father quit his job and the family formed a not-for-profit organization called Trevor's Place, which continues to spread its outreach today.

Surprise can happen to institutions, too. The pastor and leaders of the United Church of Christ in Norwell, Massachusetts, saw the writing on the wall: to survive, this congregation had to empower and train lay people for the day when there would not be enough ordained clergy or enough money to pay clergy. But as the pastor Dr. Stephen Chapin Garner and lay leaders like Jerry Thornell began to train the other lay members, who in turn began teaching and ministering, a strange thing began to happen. Gifted leaders began coming forth wanting to enter ordained ministry. In *Scattering Seeds: Cultivating Church Vitality*, Garner and Thornell tell of the surprise reversal: "We had a plan, we had a goal, we had an end result in mind, and our efforts had an effect that we never intended. In an attempt to create a clergy-free church, we wound up creating clergy that are now serving local churches in our area."[3]

Gratitude

Open my eyes
to see the joys—
the gratitudes that rise
from suffering and surprise.

RESILIENCE

To become empowered is to renew the quality of the healthy, resilient child within the elder. Resilience has to do with encountering obstacles, and prayer is the laboratory that transforms the barriers into bridges of passion and compassion. Resurrection translates into the quality of resilience: when life knocks you down, whatever enables you to bounce back with gratitude and compassion can rightly be called prayer.

RISK AND FEAR

To risk following your passion brings a kind of holy fear. "Scared to Life!" I once titled an Easter sermon based on the end of Mark's Gospel, where women leave the empty tomb afraid (Mark 16:1–8). At the thirty-fourth Kennedy Center Honors, world-renowned cellist Yo-Yo Ma said, "I'm not brave. Actually I'm pretty scared a lot of the time. But I must like being scared because I keep doing things that scare me." Though spoken amid the glitz of Hollywood icons and prestigious awards, that is honest to God prayer.

Praying into your fear can be a way to unearth powerful energy within the fear itself. The Swiss physician-writer Paul Tournier was once asked how he helped his patients get rid of their fears. He answered famously, "I don't"—because anything worthwhile is scary. By avoiding fear they would also avoid the beauty of reality; he wanted to help people experience reality. In the fairy tale "Beauty and the Beast," only when Beauty embraces the monster does her fear transform into awesome, loving power.

The Tree of Life: Paradigm of Balancing

A tree's circumference is never perfectly symmetrical, with leaves above and roots beneath ground. Once, I was writing about the tree as a spiritual metaphor and a forestry consultant interrupted me to look at a two-hundred-year-old tree next to my house. I thought, *Good, I can learn from him.* So I mentioned how I was writing about the tree as a paradigm for the spiritual life. He told me the realistic truth about the common misconception that the tree is perfectly balanced.

He pointed out how the street sewer and water main would have injured the root system, yet at the place of the wound the tree develops a huge breakout root. And that one new root—maybe twice the width of the tree's circumference—can supply more elements than many normal tree roots. He went on to relate this metaphor to the abused kids whom he was tutoring in an after-school program. He saw his work with the youth as a way of empowering kids to generate the breakout root.

Olympic athlete Quanitta Underwood told the *New York Times* how she found it empowering to talk about what happened in her living nightmare of her father abusing her and her sister. Her breakout root has drawn her into the unique role of being the lead contestant in women's boxing. More than that, she believes she is empowering masses of others by telling her story of transforming abuse into a positive cause.

In such a way your tree of life may evolve not with perfectly symmetrical balance but more like bonsai: the tree is pruned or wounded in such a way that it develops a kind of Zen-like unbalanced balance and beauty. As a retreatant said to me, she was not seeking balance but balancing—a continuing prayerful process.

BALANCING AND TIMING

In this spiritual tapestry, prayer that empowers the soul involves the double threads of feasting and fasting, the *via positiva* and the *via negativa*, expanding and emptying.

In primal traditions, creative youthful morning energies and noon energies give way to the afternoon and evening of life's diminishments. In Hinduism these are known as the path of desire and the path of renunciation.

You see the tension of these qualities in Jewish and Christian modes in Ecclesiastes: "For everything there is a season, and a time for every matter under heaven: a time to be born and a time to die; a time to plant, and a time to pluck up what is planted" (3:1–7). Angry prophets want to tear down what kingly and priestly leaders have spent their lives building. Jesus's tender healing of the woman who touches his robe is counterpointed by his anger as he overturns the tables of merchants who rob the poor in the temple. Prayer is about the nuanced balancing of these rhythms.

African American spirituals embody this balancing in their cryptic codes combining spiritual and political freedom. "Steal away to Jesus" was both about stealing away for spiritual refuge in the mind and heart and stealing away to freedom via the Underground Railroad. In *Harriet Tubman*, Beverly Lowery shows how this "black Moses" calculated exquisite timing for each of her passengers to "board" the railroad to freedom. It's the *wu wei* of the Tao, the art of sensing the time to act and the time not to act. Prayer has a lot to do with balancing, and balancing has a lot to do with timing and awareness.

HUMILITY AND POWER

Bold women in the Gospel portraits of Jesus serve as the archetype of courage coupled with humility: they storm the gates of heaven yet take the consequences. A widow knocks on the judge's door until finally he grants her justice. Jesus concludes, "Will not God grant justice to his chosen ones who cry out to him day and night?" (Luke 18:7). Honest to God prayer sometimes means taking the risk to storm the gates of heaven for the sake of earth.

It may seem strange to suggest that genuine humility and empowerment can be two sides of the same coin. I never understood the idea of "false humility" until I began meeting with a Catholic sister for spiritual guidance. From time to time, I would describe someone who seemed gifted, yet who consistently turned down the opportunity to use those gifts. My guide would say, "That sounds like a false humility." I finally began to get it for myself. What often looks like humility in the guise of seeming "modest" may actually mask my own lack of courage, avoiding risk and responsibility. When someone says, "I need more faith," I say, "Take more risks." Holy risk calls for bold prayer that produces humility.

> Genuine humility does not mean cowering in meekness, but rather it means taking the risk to follow your passion and offer your gifts to bless people and the world.

In *The Shawshank Redemption*, a classic movie based on Stephen King's novel, Andy Dufresne (Tim Robbins) is wrongly convicted of shooting his cheating wife and her lover. As prison librarian, he receives LP records. Locking the warden in the bathroom, Andy boldly enters the warden's office and plays a Mozart duet over the prison sound system. Prisoners inside rise from sleep; outside they stand at attention. Red (Morgan Freeman) describes the music as "so beautiful it can't be expressed in words, and makes your heart ache because of it.... It was like some beautiful bird flapped into our drab little cage and made these walls dissolve away ... and for the briefest of moments—every last man at Shawshank felt free." Then Freeman's voice announces that Andy "got two weeks in the hole for that stunt."

As this story shows, genuine humility does not mean cowering in meekness, but rather it means taking the risk to follow your passion and offer your gifts to bless people and the world. Real humility follows in the way of Gandhi or King, Eleanor Roosevelt or Rosa Parks. Love frees you to claim your gifts and offer them to the world, at the risk of being thrown into a dark hole of being misunderstood.

In a reverse way, then, empowerment can be an expression of genuine humility, the courage to follow where Love leads you, to offer your gifts to the world, regardless of the consequences.

The Power of Questions

Sometimes your vocational passion is born out of a deep questioning of the way things are, so that you can discover a new way things can be. Sometimes questioning the path can lead you to a new path.

Questions can also ignite energy to claim new possibilities in your present work. Thirty-something Sean told of a recent shift in his management team. It all started when Sean's sixty-something friend Keith e-mailed him an Internet link, "The Art of Powerful Questions," and Sean forwarded it to his team. "Now," he says, "instead of beginning our weekly meetings with problems we need to solve, we've been starting with questions. Converting problems into creative questions has shifted the tone of our meetings."

Scientific discovery and practical invention are born out of someone questioning the status quo of accepted worldviews and practices. Galileo questioned the geocentric universe; Gandhi questioned Eurocentric colonialism; Susan B. Anthony and Lucretia

Mott questioned male authority; Martin Luther King Jr. questioned ingrained patterns of segregation; physicist Werner Heisenberg questioned Einstein in trying to understand subatomic particles. In embracing their dreams, each one experienced the humility of cultural resistance as a result of questioning the status quo.

The process of discerning your vocation beneath your career often involves an upheaval of uncertainty, a period of questioning.

In *Kitchen Table Wisdom*, Rachel Naomi Remen, MD, tells of a time in her life when she received a major promotion at Stanford's School of Medicine: "A hundred other physicians would kill to step into my shoes. I desperately wanted to accept the promotion, but something held me back." Remen had begun to question Western modalities of curing versus Eastern wisdom of healing. "Could people have an intuitive sense of the direction of their healing? Did our relationship to our patients affect outcome as profoundly as our medications?"

She gave herself some time by visiting her family in Florida. Sitting in silence on a park bench on the afternoon of her birthday, she and her mother noticed a child drawing faces on her fingertips with a magic marker. Her mother asked, did Rachel remember as a child drawing on her hands? No, she didn't. "You would take your daddy's fountain pen and draw eyes in the palms of your hands. Then you would hold your hands up on either side of your face with your palms facing forward.... You would close your eyes and say, '*Now* I can see you,' and giggle. Such a funny thing," her mother said.

A friend had recently given Remen the poetry and artwork of Kahlil Gibran in *The Prophet*, which had a drawing of a hand with a gentle and compassionate human eye in its palm—a traditional Hindu symbol for the healer. Remen writes, "On an average day in the pediatric clinics, I washed my hands thirty or forty times. Perhaps over the years, I had washed away my eyes. About two weeks later, I resigned from Stanford and began looking for my lost eyes."[4]

Questions lie at the heart of spiritual direction, which is a prayerful conversation between the guide and the companion. Waiting for a stoplight at a five-point intersection near Hershey, Pennsylvania, I thought, *I could turn right and go see Sister Marion (my spiritual director) about a troubling situation.* But by the time the light turned green, I knew the question she would ask me. I drove straight home.

I knew the question she would ask: not what she would tell me—not advice or answers. For me, that moment offers a paradigm for spiritual companioning: the direction begins to happen within the soul of the seeker. Such guidance opens up rather than closes down the spirit of the guide and the seeker.

If gratitude is the rich soil that virtues grow out of, then questioning works up the soil so the seed can germinate. We are back to psalm-like praying, where the yin and yang of thanksgiving and questioning, even with another human being, can become an unconscious prayer to empower a vocation.

The Question

> The question you asked
> out of nowhere
> set me to the task.

> But I didn't find out
> till years later
> what I was about.

CHAPTER FOUR

Embracing Dreams

The Process of Empowerment

Follow your bliss.
—JOSEPH CAMPBELL, *THE POWER OF MYTH*

The place God calls you to is the place where your deep
gladness and the world's deep hunger meet.
—FREDERICK BUECHNER, *WISHFUL THINKING*

The soul among all creatures is generative, like God is.
—MEISTER ECKHART

*E*mpowering prayer means claiming your gifts and embracing your half-
buried dreams for the sake of the world. This is mountain-moving
prayer where all things are possible with God. How does this process
of empowerment follow from noticing, offering, and listening? As we
saw in the caveat of Rachel Naomi Remen's story, if you try to claim
your gifts without listening to your deepest passion and dreams, you
risk claiming raw power or latching onto surface abilities without
discerning your deeper spiritual gifts and vocational calling.

The deepening process of prayer empowers you to embrace your
dreams of who you can be in the world. Your vocation is your unique

microchip for "mending the universe" or "repairing the world"—
tikkun olam in the Jewish tradition. It's a call to mend concentric
layers of the universe: to create healing environments with God,
self, neighbor, nations, world, and all things. Sexuality is the basic
ingredient in our conception, birth, and life on earth, and it's the
source and expression of our deepest longings and yearnings, which
feed directly into our unique way of mending the world.

Sexuality and Vocation: Intimacy and Generativity

*Sexuality is our divinely given desire for loving, life-giving intimacy that
nurtures all spheres of life, though often abused, and often misunderstood only
as physical expression.*

Growing up not far from Intercourse, Pennsylvania, as a youth I
enjoyed all the jokes and puns about sex. *Intercourse* in original English
usage can refer to communication and intimate conversation, but also
to the interchange of goods and commerce. Through such associations,
a public marker indicates, the small town in Lancaster County got its unique name. (Only in recent centuries did the specifically sexual use of the term occur.)

We desperately crave spiritual intimacy beyond our physical loves and spiritual fulfillment beyond our routine work. What stories embody that for you?

We long for intercourse in multiple layers of life: for intimate communication and communion in our relationships with people and with divine Love;
for meaningful interchanges in our work that connect us with a sense
of purpose and vocation. Such connections expand and empower the
spiritual understanding of sexuality in life-giving ways, creating a
sense of communion in everyday communication.

Generativity, creative fruit-bearing beyond oneself, has deep
spiritual roots. "The soul among all creatures is generative, like God

is," said medieval mystic Meister Eckhart. He said God is giving birth all the time, and that is our work too. We're called to bear fruits of love.

"To love and to work"—so psychiatrist Sigmund Freud described twin aspects of human life. In a sex-saturated and economically driven culture, we spend most of our energies on relationships and work. Sex and work are two areas of our body's deepest passion and pain. We desperately crave spiritual intimacy beyond our physical loves and spiritual fulfillment beyond our routine work. What stories embody that for you?

We all knew the open secret of my high school English teacher, Miss Laura Long: her only love died in World War I. She had no children—except thousands of us students. Walking down the aisle, she would gesture, "Now that's what Shakespeare says. But Kent, what is *your* philosophy of life?" I'm still living into the answer. Here's a transforming spiritual mystery. How many anonymous nuns and monks quietly transform disillusioned sexual intimacy into countless ways that create intimate exchanges and creative commerce to bless the world?

TERRIFIC AND TERRIFYING

In primal traditions, the noon of life in the direction of the South celebrates youthful passion as sexual, familial, and vocational energies come alive. The sun is upward, the time for achieving. In high-tech culture, the daily deluge of electronic communications often derails our passion and compassion, so we crave safe, spiritual intimacy. The connection of sexuality with spirituality is as exhilarating and frightening as Everest. It is a terrific thing—terrific as in wonderful, yet terrifying.

Our erotic energies are integrally related to our deepest longings, sufferings, and joys. Healthy spirituality is all about naming, validating, and transforming human experiences of joy *and* pain. Only then can our whole selves—broken and blessed—become vessels of Love. Sexuality is a sacred, terrific gift, to be guarded and celebrated: lovingly and responsibly, safely and gently. Even when we are abused or unfulfilled, sex can become the source of spiritual transformation.

The Persian Sufi poet Hafiz began his spiritual journey by glimpsing a beautiful young woman in Shiraz. He was a poor baker boy and she was already promised to a nobleman. Nevertheless, Hafiz began composing love poems, which became popular all over Persia. Then Hafiz made a deal with God: he would keep a forty-night vigil at the tomb of a famous saint if he could win this lovely woman. But at daybreak on the fortieth day, the archangel Gabriel appeared gloriously to Hafiz. If God's messenger was so beautiful, how much more beautiful must God be! Hafiz had fallen in love with Love.

GENERATIVITY AS FRUITFULNESS

In a world that recently marked seven billion inhabitants on planet Earth, the concept of spiritual generativity can reframe the reproductive aspect of human sexuality. Sex and work are so intimately related because our real work is to express creative love in all of life.

In the Genesis creation story, the command "Be fruitful and multiply" is not just about making babies. Biblically, to be created "in the image of God" is a call to bear the fruit of love in personal, familial, vocational, and global spheres of life (see Genesis 1:26–28).

A focused vocation creates a healthy way of expressing intimacy and generativity with the world. Writers, artists, and scientists know this: you conceive an idea, it gestates, you carry it, you may feel sick and weary of holding it, then finally through pain it's delivered to the world.

Ordinary persons may exude extraordinary generativity. Over the seventy-eight years of her working lifetime, Osceola McCarty, a poor African American, saved her meager income from doing wealthier people's laundry. When she retired in 1995, she left a $150,000 trust to the University of Southern Mississippi—taking joy in the first recipient's success.

Your life mission is a key for living awake to your passion to bear the fruit of compassion. In *Teaching a Stone to Talk*, Annie Dillard describes the process of giving yourself to your own cause: "I think it would be well, and proper, and obedient, and pure, to grasp your one necessity and not let it go, to dangle from it limp wherever it takes you." Maybe this is Kierkegaard's prayer as necessity—breathing out and dangling limp while embracing your dream with passion and compassion.

Designing Your Life Mission: Balancing Focus and Freedom

A single focus for your life creates a healing of purpose for your soul and the world. It's your unique expression in a few words that link your heart with the Word of love beating in the heart of the world's chaos. The Ignatian question is, what brings God glory by making you fully alive to your life's purpose? I invite you to design or redesign your life mission after reading through this chapter (see Prayer Practice 12).

FOCUSING

Your life mission is your unique purpose for mending the universe.

When filmmaker Dan Karslake heard a single line in a lecture— that every three seconds someone in the world dies of preventable causes—his passion ignited, again. He was already traveling full speed with his award-winning film *For the Bible Tells Me So*, which aims to promote openness for gays and lesbians. But that same passion and empathy to emanate unlimited possibilities now fuels his new documentary *Every Three Seconds*, which seeks to change the face of world poverty.

A life mission statement is your platform for leaning into life's stress to create what I call playful projects for serious purposes. It's harnessing that twin combination of what brings you joy with some pain in the world. "The surf that distresses the ordinary swimmer produces in the surf-rider the super-joy of going clean through it," says early YMCA leader Oswald Chambers. By focusing, you're not ignoring the chaos and resistance but using it.

"The person with a *why* to live can endure almost any *how*"— almost any circumstances. That's how Viktor Frankl, imprisoned in a death-dealing concentration camp, distilled the wisdom of survivors in his classic book *Man's Search for Meaning*. Jesus says, "If your eye is focused, your whole body will be full of light" (Matthew 6:22, AT). Your life mission is your why to live, the focus that floods your life with light.

> With focus, our cycling around and fallings and risings spiral into a joyous life mission.

In the film *Billy Elliot*, Billy falls as he tries to dance. His teacher tells him to keep his eye on a spot on the wall—and it becomes an eloquent dance between focus and freedom. With focus, our cycling around and fallings and risings spiral into a joyous life mission.

GERMINATING

A young man who served in Africa working for peace and justice concerns told of visiting King Tutankhamen's tomb. He fell into conversation with an elderly security guard on his last day at the job. He had been present decades ago, he confided, when grain had been found in the tomb—and had taken a few kernels home. He planted the ancient seed, and it produced grain until the present.

Within each of us is the seed of a unique purpose. In *The Soul's Code*, James Hillman uses such an image: that in each of us lies an acorn with a distinctive script. But when the acorn cracks, how do you discern if the script that unfolds is true to your unique soul— what for me is the Christ-self?

Mighty Whole

> The oak draws down strength from
> the sky, the rain, the sun,
> deepening its life in the
> Ground of its being,
> as at the very
> beginning
> a tiny
> acorn
> falling,
> lying,
> waiting,
> then bursting,
> breaking, oaking,
> lost itself to become
> a greater Self in the Mighty Whole.

Testing Your Life Mission: Discerning Life's Choices

Like the grain in King Tut's tomb, an acorn buried in the human soul can contain a miniature word of Love. Only when an acorn breaks open can it become the oak it is meant to be. As the soul's acorn cracks, if you pay attention, it can guide you to your true north to stay in the flow of the Spirit's leading. Like four points of a compass, you can test a true direction from a false direction through integrity of inner-outer passion, childhood epiphanies, patterns in your stories, and clues in your dreams.

INNER-OUTER INTEGRITY

"Follow your bliss," the world's great mythologist Joseph Campbell said over and over. (People misquote Campbell—"Find your bliss"—finders keepers, got it in my pocket!) *Follow* is a disciple word in all spiritual streams, conveying a process, a pilgrimage with obstacles;

your means it's a path with your unique DNA and life experiences; *bliss*—change one letter and you get *bless*: Will your life mission issue in blessing or destruction?

That's the acid test of your life mission. Hitler's passion did not arise from bliss; it issued in destruction. Test specific calls within your mission: look for traces of the yin and yang of your inner and outer passion. In essayist Frederick Buechner's words, "where your deep gladness and the world's deep hunger meet." In a retreat I led in Manhattan, when participants returned from meditating in Central Park, we all sat in awe when a young Greenwich Village artist shared his life mission: "I am here on this earth to be a steward of God's dreams...." How would that get you awake every morning?

CHILDHOOD EPIPHANIES

Revisiting the dreamy stuff of your youthful years can provide a laboratory for testing your life mission. When Rachel Naomi Remen was trying to discern whether to accept the promotion at Stanford's School of Medicine, in a serendipitous moment, her mother reminded her how as a child she used to draw eyes on the palms of her hands, an ancient Hindu symbol of healing. The hidden childhood epiphany made her choice clear.

Around age seven, Lela climbed a windmill on her family's Nebraska farm. When her father discovered her, he screamed, "Lela, come down right now! Whatever are you doing? That's dangerous!" The child said, "But I wanted to see the whole world!" No wonder: eventually she would see the world, serving as a missionary educator in South Asian countries with her husband for more than forty years.[1]

But sometimes following your bliss means following your blisters, as a friend said. Your dream may lead like switchbacks on a mountain climbing expedition, through difficult twists and turns as you pray your way to the summit.

In *Joseph and His Technicolor Dreamcoat*, Andrew Lloyd Webber dramatizes the longest single story in the Hebrew Bible (Genesis

37–50). Joseph's ego-centered youthful epiphanies escalate family dysfunction and sibling jealousy, yet they get woven into a redeeming vocation. Joseph's brothers sell him into slavery in Egypt. But mysteriously his bad trip is used for good. Later during a famine, Joseph, now elevated as Pharaoh's vice regent, starts a world food program for alien Egyptians and his own alienated kinsfolk; in a painful reconciliation the family comes home in a strange land. Joseph's story weaves together the themes of sexuality and generativity, humility and vocation, comedy and hospitality in a powerful summation of providence: "Even though you intended to do harm to me, God intended it for good" (Genesis 50:20).

"The best way to distinguish between a false story and a true one, or between a counterfeit and an authentic call, is to compare the present experience of your story or vocation with the dreams of your youth," writes Marc Gafni in *Soul Prints*. Too often, for the sake of success or in the wake of hardship, we give up on a dream of our youth, when, like the seed in King Tut's tomb, there still may be a season for it to germinate, even if in an unpredictable form.

PATTERNS IN STORIES

Our ancestors charted their course by the stars and created stories from the shapes of constellations. Patterns in our stories have power to shape our lives and allow us to embrace our dreams. The mark of a life-giving story often involves a downturn into an impasse followed by an upturn into some fruit born of the struggle. But the experience may embody a movement from the White House to a log cabin as often as the other way around.

Vacationing on Cape Cod, I got my two-year-old daughter her first kite. Blue with a white Egyptian ankh, a symbol of life, it flew beautifully—until it got snarled in a tree. I gave up. I moseyed to my car and started to leave. Then, I stopped. I went back. Whether from a gust (*Geist*—German for Spirit) of wind or from my gentle tug on the string, I don't know, but the kite miraculously untangled itself. It's a paradigm for my life. When things get tangled, I need to retreat to relinquish my tight grasp. If it comes back, it's a gift. For me, touchstone experiences often involve a twist of giving up and returning, each equally empowering in its own time.

I discovered another pattern through journaling with a dream: my most fulfilling experiences come through a combination of priming the pump myself and God's grace through the back door. Pounding on the front door often gets me in trouble. I invite you to try connecting your touchstone experiences to the arc of stories in your life and in your own spiritual tradition.

DREAMING AWAKE

We often forfeit our dreams for the sake of other's expectations, a career path, financial stability, or wanting to act normal. What's normal? Primal culture or ours? On the day of Pentecost the apostle Peter quotes the Jewish prophet Joel, "Your youth shall see visions and your elders shall dream dreams" (Joel 2:28; Acts 2:17, AT).

During lunch break on retreat, a woman wrote on newsprint, "Who's stealing the elders' dreams?" I added, "Who's stealing the visions of our youth?" Martin Luther King Jr.'s "I Have a Dream" speech still calls us to value the content of a person's character beyond class or color, with nonviolent actions for peace and justice. Can you reignite your dreams?

By dreaming awake I mean paying attention to your sleep dreams as friends of the soul that are trying to say, Wake up! I also mean being so alert during waking hours that you pay attention to the sting of a friend's comment, a luminous tree by the highway, the distraction of a tailgater, a fantasy you've tried to push aside—or your dream vocation. It's Trevor Farrell being moved to compassion by a TV clip showing a homeless man in Philadelphia. It's Brother Lawrence seeing a tree barren in winter echoing his soul—soon to burst into bloom.

> Can you reignite your dreams?

Dreams are signals to wake up to your soul's need for *warnings* (brake lights), *reassurances* (night-lights), and *maintenance* (dash lights). These three signals serve your greater quest for the "grail" of life— as in the legend of the Holy Grail: dreams of *invitation* and *vocation* (headlights). Or they point to minicalls within the call, specific invitations for living out your life mission.

All four may intertwine: a frightening warning may be an invitation to action, and the most luminous invitation may scare you to the bones. To follow an impossible dream, you need all the reassurances and healthy maintenance you can get, so as to not go off course. And when you find your golden grail, you drink from it in order to give to others.

Folks ignore awful dreams when they may bear awesome rustlings of Eternity. At age fifty C. S. Lewis had lost his zeal for writing; he thought he would be remembered as a once-famous writer who would die unknown. Then he began having nightmares about lions. They attacked Lewis's lethargy. Writing feverishly, he published *The Lion, the Witch and the Wardrobe* that same year—quickly followed by six other Narnian stories. The Lion seemed to come out of nowhere.

Once during an intense time of church conflict, a disgruntled couple appeared in one of my dreams. *This complaining wife and husband are planting a palm tree just outside the south door of the historic church where I am pastor (but would soon leave); next, they are installing a computer system in the church office. I feel mysteriously joyous.*

Three years later I reread the dream with a start. By then I had founded a not-for-profit organization, Oasis Ministries for Spiritual Development, and created, as our logo, a palm tree showing its roots in rippling water. Why the south door? In the Native prayer in four directions (that I had begun to practice daily), the South represents the noon of one's vocational energies, rejuvenating my spirit at the point of a midlife desert crisis at age forty-five. Shortly after that, the computer shows up: *I dream my computer catches fire while I'm writing my first book—and I try dousing it with water.* Writing had become my new pulpit. The disgruntled "angels" were unwitting headlights on my vocational path.

Living awake to your soul's integrity, epiphanies, stories, and dreams renews physical and mental health, sheds light on relationships, and aids in discerning vocational choices. (After reading the prayer poem, return to Prayer Practice 12). Let this desire only guide your choices: What brings God glory by making you more fully alive to your life's purpose? In poetic form, here is Ignatius's process of discerning how to serve fully alive.

Choosing Well, Living Whole

Sometimes choosing is like
a ship going straight to port:
no hesitation or negotiation:
the heart's Desire is clear.

Sometimes choosing is like
sailing with an untoward wind—
the pulls of consolations,
the counter-pulls of desolations.
But, Ah! You tack into the stress;
with skill you follow your bliss.

Other times there's no movement.
You're dead in the water: you yearn
for disturbance or assurance yet
get only deafening echoes of apathy.

Then is when you take the challenge
to chart an inner course to change:
gather information—facts and feelings;
picture the choice in your mind's eye,
then weigh its pros and cons.

Imagine a colleague in your shoes,
what do you say to help the person choose?
Imagine yourself at the end of life:
what choice gives inward peace, less strife?
With Gandhi, picture the poorest person
in the world—then make your decision.

Present your self wholly to God:
How does this choice sit
with your head, your heart,
and the pattern of your faith journey?

Practices for Cultivating Empowerment

Group Experiment with Focusing Energies

Try this experiment with a small group. Ask for a volunteer to sit in the center of the circle, blindfolded. Request the rest of the group to focus their energies on the one in the center. In a few minutes, give a silent signal to release the focus. Wait a minute. Then ask the blindfolded person (who usually feels the shift) to report. Ask: If we can experience normal human energies across a room, why not in Germany? Or Ghana? Were they thinking of love as they focused their energies? What are the connections with prayer or meditation?

Prayer Practice 8

Breathing as Prayer

Pause now, and breathe slowly, deeply. Imagine inhaling as receiving the gift of life … then exhaling as giving back…. Enjoy the rhythm of receiving … giving…. Notice your chest rising … falling … expanding … emptying…. Imagine breathing the same air that sustains animals and humans, trees and sea creatures, rich and poor. Spend a few minutes praying in this manner for trees that conserve the environment, for all races who breathe the same air, for loved ones near or far. Then offer audible groans or sighs on behalf of suffering people in the news or friends with heavy burdens: *ahhh*…. End by contemplating a beautiful sunrise or sunset with a few joyous sighs: *ahhh!!!* The same primal sound becomes a prayer for suffering—or for rejoicing! Sense your body's gratitude for the rhythm of life. (For sighing as wordless prayer, see Romans 8:26.)

Prayer Practice 9

Kything Prayer

Kythe in Old English means to "feel close to"; as folks say, "they're kith and kin." Kything is a way to practice the gift of imagination. Visualizing another person as complete, their countenance uplifted, is an empowering way to pray without words, "holding the person in the Light," a Quaker phrase. Pause now … slow down your breathing … allow the face of someone you love to come to mind. Center, and picture the person you want to pray for in the Light: Hold their face in your mind's eye. Now try placing your arms and hands in an X shape across your chest for several minutes, holding her or him in your heart (see Philippians 1:7). Finally, exhale while dropping your hands … releasing your loved one to the arms of God, letting go—the hardest job parents or caregivers have.

Prayer Practice 10

The *Lectio* Process in All of Life

The Benedictine method for reading and meditating with scripture, *lectio divina* (literally "divine reading"), provides a transferable spiritual practice to sharpen your vision in all of life, to meditate on a moment of awareness that either *delights* or *disturbs* you. Take a walk or a ride, meet with someone, read a poem, see a movie, or recall a dream—with special intention simply to be aware of sounds and surroundings (voices, music, wind, sunlight, foliage, rain, rocks). Notice a moment that arrests your attention: a line of a conversation or a movie scene, a dream fragment or an experience of nature. Sit for a few minutes in silence, simply being with that experience.

Option: Open your journal to a clean page or to a new document on your computer, and begin to write, recalling as many here-and-now particulars as possible. When you put down your pen or pencil—or pull back from the keypad—read over what you've written, underlining or highlighting "luminous particulars"— phrases, metaphors, or images. Read it aloud to someone, or ask a person to read it to you. Reflect again on poignant images; choose one and meditate on it in silence. Do you sense any new insight for your life?

Prayer Practice 11

Your Own Portable Monastery

After working for some time on the phone, at the computer, or on another project, push your chair back a few inches, with your lap and hands empty. Take a few deep breaths … let a line of a poem, scripture, or a sacred word come to mind (see Prayer Practice 4). You have entered your portable monastery. After a minute or so, pull your chair back to your work area … and continue working.

Option: Place an icon, a singing bowl, or chime at your workspace; push back to meditate on the icon or the sound of the bowl or chime. (A group example: try this exercise during a committee or group meeting.) For further meditation, I offer these words from the Alcoholics Anonymous *Big Book*:

> As we go through the day we pause, when agitated or doubtful, and ask for the right thought or action. We constantly remind ourselves we are no longer running the show, humbly saying to ourselves many times each day "Thy will be done."* We are then in much less danger of excitement, fear, anger, worry, self-pity, or foolish decisions. We become much more efficient. We do not tire so easily for we are not burning up energy foolishly as we did when we were trying to arrange life to suit ourselves.[2]

*Or repeat a few centering words of your own.

Prayer Practice 12

Designing Your Life Mission

Meditate with Frederick Buechner's words: "The place God calls you to is the place where your deep gladness and the world's deep hunger meets." On a clean page in your journal or a new document on your computer, write: *I am here on this earth to*…. Pause. Let your mission statement reflect this two-fold focus: What puts a sparkle in your eyes (your deep gladness)? What pulls at your heartstrings (some deep hunger of the world)? Avoid being too general (to love everyone) or too specific (to lay bricks). Put your flesh on your mission with the words *through* or *by*: "to express love through the building blocks of my life, or by creating…." For a youth, your mission can guide you for decades to come; for an elder, it can flood past decades with meaning. Word it in a way that speaks to employment, retirement, or disability. Keep it short; express it in a sentence. Rework your mission; repeat it as a prayer of your heart; put it on a card inside your closet, desk, or wallet.

Method: Reread your opening stem: *I am here on this earth to....* Pause for a couple of minutes, repeating this phrase as your heart's prayer, to be present to your self, and God, and the world. Begin to write. When you stop, read what you've written once; then a second time highlight or underline luminous phrases that leap out at you. Condense the highlights to one vital sentence. (Incorporate other aspects as goals or objectives.)

Option: Use art to express your life mission. Let an image or metaphor arise that encapsulates the essence of your life mission. Experiment with a non-linear way to express it in art ... chalk ... pastels ... clay ... poetry ... music ... or movement.

Prayer as Relinquishment

Emptying

CHAPTER FIVE

Negative Capability

The Grounding for Relinquishment

> One cannot live the afternoon of life according to the
> program of life's morning; for what was great in the
> morning will be of little importance in the evening,
> and what in the morning was true will at evening have
> become a lie.
>
> —CARL JUNG, *THE STRUCTURE AND DYNAMICS OF THE PSYCHE*

> At every moment we see diminishment, both in us
> and around us ... premature deaths, stupid accidents,
> weaknesses affecting the highest reaches of our being.
> How can these diminishments ... become for us a
> source of good?
>
> —TEILHARD DE CHARDIN, *THE DIVINE MILIEU*

In the afternoon of life in the direction of the West, necessity tempers possibility: dreams encounter limits. You've awakened and now you're focused, but you can be too focused on this moment, which soon becomes that moment. That's why spiritual teachers speak of detachment, relinquishing the experience you just had so that you can be open to the one that's waiting for you in this moment.

Relinquishment shows up in stories and metaphors of almost all spiritual streams. In the Hebrew Bible, prayer as relinquishment means you're like Abraham laying your hopes for Isaac on the altar; you're like Joseph the dream kid now sitting in prison; you're like Moses who's not allowed to enter the land of promise: dreams seem to have died. The Sufi Shams throws his soul friend Rumi's treasured books into the river. The Buddhist practice of *maranasati*, "death meditation," parallels "dying with Christ" in the Christian Scriptures.

As in an ancient Eastern parable, if you hold the bird too tightly, you'll kill it. If you release your grasp, and it flies away never to come back, it wasn't really yours. If it comes back, you receive it as a gift and hold it lightly.

When the resurrected Jesus appears to Mary Magdalene in the garden, she thinks he's the gardener. That's how mundane spirituality is: embodied Love reverberates in the guise of a gardener (or a chef or an advice-giving fisher). Then the moment Mary knows who it is, Jesus says an amazing thing to her: "Do not hold on to me" (John 20:17).

A story from the Buddha illustrates the dangers of holding on to your ideas and experiences too tightly.

> While a young widower is away on business, bandits burn his village. On returning, the widower finds the remains of a dead child near his former house. Assuming it is his own son, after proper cremation ceremonies, he carries the remains with him at all times, continually grieving. But in fact his son has been kidnapped. One night the real son escapes and comes to his father's new house, pounding on the door, "Papa, it's me, open the door." "But," the father insists, "you cannot be my son; my son is dead." He will not open the door—and his son leaves, never to be embraced by his own father.[1]

Honest to God prayer means being willing to give up preconceived ideas to open the door to truth. To really listen to your life as you follow your bliss, you need to become agnostic—literally "unknowing." So the anonymous fourteenth-century English Christian classic *The Cloud of Unknowing* would invite us to be still and unlearn, to relinquish ego-centered certainty and experience a naked trust in God.

Struggling with Relinquishment

You may struggle with prayer as empowerment because power seems at odds with the traditional message of self-denial and humility. But prayer as relinquishment presents an even greater struggle, because pathological religion distorts spirituality into extreme self-denial. Many people see classical mystics as promoting a "hair shirt" theology instead of seeing the treasure of their freedom from self as freedom for Self.

We struggle with the concept of relinquishing, letting go. Even well-meaning, enlightened persons misuse the phrase "let go." Imagine telling a family with a suicide or a person who's suddenly disabled, "You just need to let go of that!" Yet that's the subtle cruel message that comes through all too often for persons whose losses may be less dramatic. Somehow the word *relinquish* has a gentler flow, conveying more of a sense of unfolding. Try saying aloud, "Let go." Notice how crisp the words sound. Now say, "Relinquish...." Feel all the air leaving your body.

Another barrier to the idea of relinquishment and its cousin emptiness is that in industrialized technological civilizations we're taught to fill every space—produce, do something useful: "Don't just stand there, do something!" Like the Buddha, try turning it on its head; say it backwards: "Don't just do something, stand there." If you lose your spiritual center and balance, the Tao of yin and yang, you may be flailing your arms in midair like a drowning person who doesn't

> Honest to God prayer means being willing to give up preconceived ideas to open the door to truth.

know how to swim. The art of prayer is learning how to practice the vital balance of action and nonaction in troubled waters.

How can we find life-giving metaphors of this built-in need for relinquishment and emptiness? Gerald May, my mentor at Shalem Institute, used to say, "Everything I let go of has my claw marks all over it." As a psychiatrist and spiritual guide, May modeled playful, realistic spiritual honesty.

Rhythms in the Body and Nature

Nature's rhythms, with the path of the sun's rising and setting and the seasons waxing and waning, and the body's rhythms and breathing invite us to pay attention to downward movements in our lives. French paleontologist and theologian Teilhard de Chardin asks the right question in *The Divine Milieu*: How can these diminishments become for us a source of good? While eldering means gaining in years and wisdom, the sun's light is declining, and as you age you encounter diminishments.

If you only inhale without exhaling, you will die, as Kierkegaard illustrates with his analogy of breathing and praying. The rhythm of emptying is vital to the rhythm of expanding. The chest rises and falls, and falling is a metaphor for the afternoon of life, in the direction of the West, where the shadows lengthen, and the evening comes, and the busy world is hushed—just before the nightfall (see theme IV). Authentic prayer is built into these rhythms of our body and of nature. Pause now, and take a deep breath … then exhale…. Notice your chest rising and falling.

First we'll look at Jung's metaphor, that in the afternoon of life your shadow comes to the foreground; second, at the metaphor of rising and falling; and third, at the metaphor of emptiness as negative capability.

THE THEOLOGY OF CHIAROSCURO
I'm sitting in a whitewashed room at Casa del Sol, a hermitage on the grounds of Ghost Ranch in the desert near Abiquiu, New Mexico,

where I'm on a praying writing retreat. As part of the praying, I walk past the artist Georgia O'Keeffe's studio a quarter-mile down the gravel road, or I peruse books of her amazing paintings and photos by her husband, Alfred Stieglitz.

Like every artist, O'Keeffe knew that power resides in awareness. Printed on an American commemorative stamp are her words, "Nobody sees a flower—really—it is so small—we haven't time, and to see takes time, like to have a friend takes time." Nobody sees, so she painted the tiniest flower huge so you have to slow down and notice it.

She was also aware of the power of playing with light and dark. O'Keeffe would paint brilliant red desert mesas silhouetted with deep purples and layers of shadows. Just as Rembrandt used darks and lights in his portraits to highlight the features of personality, O'Keeffe gave personality to her vistas through use of chiaroscuro, literally "light dark," the arrangement of lights and darks. But in Italian *oscuro* hints that things appear obscure, hidden.

In the afternoon of life you experience what I call the "theology of chiaroscuro." As Jung says, "One cannot live the afternoon of life according to the program of life's morning." You begin to value shadow as well as light, vulnerability as well as strength. Literally, if you're in the desert's afternoon heat, the shadow of the rock is your friend. Like the Hebrew prophet Isaiah, you welcome a Voice that says: "I will give you the treasures of darkness, riches hidden in secret places" (45:3). Or, like the apostle Paul, you hear, "My grace is sufficient, for power is made perfect in weakness" (2 Corinthians 12:9). You discover a new form of empowerment—growing down instead of up.

I suppose nothing would bring one's shadow to the foreground more than being incarcerated. Teaching writing in prison has brought home to me that the afternoon of life is not just an issue for midlife. Here's what one woman in her twenties wrote in response to an exercise in my book *Writing Tides*, "How is life like or unlike kindergarten or nursery school?"

> To me it all depends on what stage you're at in life, how mature
> you are. At one point, nothing is like kindergarten and I think
> that's when a person first gets freedom, and they think they know
> it all. After that stage, life turns back into being like kindergarten
> because you realize there's still so much you need to learn.

These rhythms are not always chronological. By reflecting on her
youthful shadow, the twenty-something woman in prison is expressing beauty through the art of her writing. A child may experience
brief moments of bliss—or wounding. Awareness of the shadow
starts much earlier than commonly accepted: witness experiences
of teen suicides and abused children. "It is an illusion that youth
are happy, an illusion of those who have lost it," wrote Somerset
Maugham in *Of Human Bondage*. In prolonged periods of illness in my
youth, a minister's wife brought me books that turned me toward
literature, poetry, music, and the arts—gifts out of my childhood
shadow.

   The theology of chiaroscuro is a spiritual skill available at any age:
it's the art of learning to develop beauty in your shadow, maybe with
O'Keeffe as your mentor. At age four, my grandson was coached to
paint after Georgia's shadowed "Poppies" and Vincent van Gogh's
luminous "Starry Night." Maybe it was preparatory training for his
soul—and remedial training for mine.

LEARNING TO FALL—AND FAIL

Attention to your own body's breathing can teach you to honor both
equally—the rhythms of rising and falling, the cycles of filling and
emptying. The great fear of someone in failing health is falling. The
two words are siblings from their Latin parent, *fallere*. Under "failure"
my computer dictionary lists "lack of success" first thing. Each of us
is constantly failing in between occasional successes. We fail tests in
school but pray for negative tests for diabetes or cancer. We fail to
live up to our own dreams and promises to others.

As a youth, Francis T. "Fay" Vincent Jr. was an outstanding athlete in track and field as well as football. But college pranksters upended his life when they locked him in his room. He climbed onto the roof, slipped and fell four stories, crushing his spine and paralyzing his legs. Against all odds he walked again, but with a limp. After a career as an entertainment lawyer and a sports executive, Fay Vincent became the eighth commissioner of Major League Baseball. He's well qualified to speak about falling and failing. In *The Spirituality of Imperfection*, Ernest Kurtz and Katherine Ketcham open with these words of Fay Vincent:

> Baseball teaches us … how to deal with failure. We learn at a very young age that failure is the norm in baseball and, precisely because we have failed, we hold in high regard those who fail less often—those who hit safely in one out of three chances and become star players. I also find it fascinating that baseball, alone in sport, considers errors to be part of the game, part of its rigorous truth.[2]

Practices of honest praying teach you to embrace diminishments in your own and other's lives, then doggedly pursue some gift in it for the life of the world. If ever scientists discover a cure or prevention for Alzheimer's disease, it will be through studying victims' diminished brains. Indeed, our widespread understanding of left and right brain functions all began by the radical severing of the two spheres of the brain to give relief to persons with severe epilepsy. I hope you who read this carry these ideas and practices into all the arenas of life, into work in health, politics, education, and science.

Malcolm Gladwell's bestselling *Outliers* may be all about what makes people successful, yet the case studies behind his wisdom consistently analyze failures—plane crashes, feuding families in Kentucky, a genius college dropout. And a failed experiment for a scientist, as Edison famously understood, is another notch on the ladder of learning.

How can reflecting on the morning and noon chapters prepare you for the afternoon of life—economic downturns, premature deaths, stupid accidents, sudden disabilities—to embrace gifts in your shadow? Beginning right now, if you practice the art of finding meaning in *being* rather than *doing* during incidents of sickness, or injury, or loss, you prepare for a higher quotient of inaction in elder years—or for surprise if life empties you at high noon. That art of finding meaning is prayer.

Emptiness as Space for New Life

All spiritual traditions have some concept of emptiness; it connects with the Sabbath: to cease, to shut down our internal computers. If we fail to claim healthy soul space, life will hand us "sabbath" in the form of a car crash or a curve ball, divorce or depression, debilitating illness or vocational crisis. Spiritual practices of East and West would tell us: Do not wait for life to empty you. Practice befriending empty spaces—bidden or unbidden—as openings for divine presence (see Prayer Practice 13).

STEPPING BACK—LIKE A JAZZ CONDUCTOR

The Hebrew Bible's opening lines in Genesis read, "The earth was a formless void, and darkness covered the face of the deep." But it's not a static void: "A wind from God swept—or brooded—over the face of the waters" just before the big bang when light exploded. Voilà! God spoke, or vibrated, "Let there be light" (Genesis 1:1–3).

> Do not wait for life to empty you.

The idea of a necessary void preceding new life lies at the heart of the kabbalistic mystical tradition of Judaism. *Tzimtzum* refers to the Creator contracting to make space for creation, like a jazz conductor stepping back so each player can solo. This stepping back creates empty space, a void where something can emerge out of nothing.

In the Christian story, the void at creation parallels Christ's self-emptying (*kenosis* in Greek). "Christ Jesus, who, though he was in the form of God ... emptied himself, taking the form of a slave, being born in human likeness ... he humbled himself and became obedient to the point of death—even death on a cross" (see Philippians 2:5–11).

The Jewish idea of *tzimtzum* and the Christian idea of *kenosis*—the self-emptying God in Christ—represent the sacrificial aspect of ongoing divine creativity.[3] Or as the ancient Hindu Rig Veda says poetically, "Sacrifice is the navel of the universe." Learn to guard emptiness as a reservoir for divine creativity and courage.

Kenosis is a movement from attachment to detachment, from mastery to Mystery. We go through the void of not knowing on the way to a new kind of knowing.

When this happens for me, I've learned to befriend the nothingness to see if it can become a bridge to new awareness. I'll write about what I can't write about. Once I had nothing to write, so I wrote about that.

Nothing

>I write about
>Nothing.
>No thing.
>Ah! No thing really
>matters,
>only relationships.

Absence morphed into presence, nothing into everything—physicists tell me that everything is about relationships. I yearn to live this truth.

Inhabiting the Mystery: Negative Capability

If we inhabit the mystery of our emptiness, we may find a treasure in the burned-out places of our lives, where, phoenix-like, the dark spaces become the next eggs of creativity. This attitude of emptiness is countercultural, valuing silence and being equally to speaking and doing. It sounds very Eastern, yet has Western counterparts: the German philosopher Lessing spoke of the value of the "creative pause." For Christians, *kenosis* means living out one's baptism, dying *and* rising in Christ. For anyone, practicing *kenosis* means relinquishing preconceived ideas—whether of self-inflation or self-deprecation—then opening yourself to surprise possibilities.

In a letter to his brother dated December 21, 1817, the poet John Keats referred to the state of unknowing as "Negative Capability." Walking home with two friends, Keats describes one of them, Dilke, as a person who has "already made up his mind about everything": he would never learn anything new. In a moment of irritation, Keats's insight dropped in.

> Several things dovetailed in my mind, and at once it struck me what quality went to form a Man of Achievement, especially in Literature & which Shakespeare possessed so enormously—I mean *Negative Capability*, that is, when man is capable of being in uncertainties, Mysteries, doubts, without an irritable reaching after fact & reason.[4]

Every creative person knows the void of unknowing as the womb for a new creation. Novelists empty their own personality in order to enter the character they write about. Maya Angelou's poetry gushed forth only after a prolonged period of self-chosen silence. Scientists halt an experiment to let an idea ferment. "Wait, I think we have touched something very important here. Let's not talk about it…. Let's wait for two weeks, and let it solve itself." So Werner Heisenberg, Nobel Prize

Powerful insights gestate unawares; do not wake them too soon. Prayer of contemplation gives birth to a life of action.

winner for his famous uncertainty principle of quantum physics, would instruct his researcher in the middle of a perplexing problem. It would solve itself. Powerful insights gestate unawares; do not wake them too soon. Prayer of contemplation gives birth to a life of action.

Slowly Goodly

When I am stressed, I think:
Goodly
things are
happening
slowly.
I thank. Then I am blessed.

CHAPTER SIX

Shedding Attachments

The Process of Relinquishment

If you will just relinquish the need to defend your point of view, you will in that relinquishment gain access to enormous amounts of energy that have been previously wasted.

—Deepak Chopra, *Seven Spiritual Laws of Success*

Those who try to make their life secure will lose it, but those who lose their life will keep it.

—Jesus, Luke 17:33

With the relinquishing of all thought and egotism, the enlightened one is liberated through not clinging.

—The Buddha, *Majjhima Nikaya* 72.15

Things end, then you spend a time (or time-out) in the neutral zone, and then things begin anew.

—William Bridges, *Transitions*

A human emergency can be the occasion for spiritual emergence. The two Chinese characters that together form the word *crisis* separately represent the words *danger* and *opportunity*. Prayer means putting on 3-D lenses to see Reality in reality.

Alfred Nobel opened a newspaper one morning to read the headline of his own obituary: *Merchant of Death Is Dead*. Actually, it was his brother who died. But the shock of realizing he would be remembered as a wealthy merchant of dynamite used for destruction and death turned his life around. Today when a Nobel Prize is given, you think of a global philanthropist for causes of science, literature, and peace. Awakened by the crisis of death, Nobel claimed his gifts to empower countless generations.

When life upends you with a surprise catastrophe, how can you carry the grounding of *kenosis* and negative capability into a lived process of relinquishment and detachment?

Pruning to Bear Fruit: The Tree of Life Again

You are meant to be generative, to bear the fruit of love. As with Nobel, fecundity can require radical pruning "to make it bear more fruit" (see John 15:1–5). "On either side of the river is the tree of life with its twelve kinds of fruit … and the leaves of the tree are for the healing of the nations" (Revelation 22:3). Ironically, your sexual passion can expand creatively as other parts of the self get pruned, fostering generativity to mend the world.

Late one afternoon I had an appointment to visit a couple, but found them behind their house. The husband was holding a quince tree while the wife was pruning its roots. The next summer that tree was bursting with fruit. Sometimes the very roots of your spiritual life get pruned; you can't pray as you once did or you don't know what you believe anymore. Good stuff—not just deadwood—even spiritual roots get pruned.

Liminal Spaces and Places

This process of detachment may happen through a crisis that hurls you into a temporary cloud of unknowing and confusion, a painful experience of pruning before new shoots of life emerge. Such transitions throw you into a spiritual fog—a liminal experience.

The word *liminal* comes from the Latin *limen,* meaning threshold—a doorway. Liminality refers to the in-between times and places, where we're temporarily emptied but opened to negative capability, a fertile limbo of the soul.

There's geographical limbo: journeying to unfamiliar places or sacred spaces can open the psyche. As Mark Twain said, "Travel is fatal to prejudice." There's social limbo: you expose yourself to the longings and experiences of marginalized people when you move out of your normal comfort zone. There's musical limbo: music transports you out of yourself to Cuba or into the song of the morning stars. There's architectural limbo: standing on a front porch or at a back door you hear yourself say something wild. There's seasonal limbo: paralleling the four directions, shifts in seasons from spring to summer to fall to winter spawn spiritual awareness. There's diurnal limbo: the fading of day to dusk, the changing of night to dawn can breed inklings of mystery. I invite you to an examen of liminal spaces in your life (see Prayer Practice 14).

CULTIVATING EMPTY SPACES

In primal cultures, elders still pass on the value of praying in nature in the evening, just as the sun sets, while there's still light in the sky, and in the early morning right before dawn. I believe these primal practices are so universal because the outward state between day and night corresponds to the inward liminal state between consciousness and unconsciousness.

People say, "It dawned on me" as they recount an insight. Such insights come indirectly. "Tell all the truth, but tell it slant," said Emily Dickinson. Try this: stand with your back to the sun in the early morning or late afternoon; experience the feeling of your elongated shadow. That's why parables and stories present truth from the backside—to wake you up to what's hidden right in front of you.

That's why REM (rapid eye movement) sleep is so fertile for dreams and insights—when dozing off or waking up. One of my mentors suggests that you not leap out of bed on awakening, but *simmer* a few minutes, allowing first thoughts to come and go without agenda, greeting the day with a grateful and open heart.

> Stand with your back to the sun in the early morning or late afternoon; experience the feeling of your elongated shadow.

You cultivate liminal potential by paying attention to night dreams (recording them when you rise) and to luminous daytime moments that create that same effect (see chapter five). Eleven-year-old Trevor Farrell was watching the *evening* news when his heart was zapped with compassion for a homeless man.

Taking risks in speaking or writing lands you on unknown turf. Carlyle Marney, a twentieth-century southern theologian with an impressive stature and voice, would expose his vulnerability as he quipped, "Whenever I can't do something, I preach about it." When you do that sort of thing, everybody's in for a surprise. We hung on his every word, because we knew it was honest to God preaching to himself.

INCUBATING INSTEAD OF ANSWERING

Liminality is a zone of ambivalence, ambiguity, even disorientation, as anthropologist Victor Turner's pioneering research shows. But it is at the same time a "realm of pure possibility where novel configurations of ideas and relations may arise." That is the value of practicing centering prayer, where you have no agenda except to empty the mind and heart of thoughts, to cultivate liminal space that leaves you prepared for surprise.

I come back to the value of questioning as prayer: first, as in the Psalms, to develop honest awareness of self, others and God; second, as in the example of Rachel Naomi Remen, to claim vocational empowerment; and third, as a way of practicing compassion for yourself and others. In *Kitchen Table Wisdom* Remen writes, "An unanswered question is a fine traveling companion. It sharpens your eye for the road."

Among the four Gospels, Jesus is asked 183 questions, directly or indirectly. How many does he answer directly? Three! By giving questions back to people, by getting them buzzing with his own questions and Zen-like parables, Jesus creates liminal spaces for churning, ruminating, incubating.

Irritation to Invitation

I feel the barbs of this little irritation,
cycling round, coursing in my veins.

Ah, is there within the irritation
some invitation I might waste
if I suppress it—or in haste express it
raw? Or let it gnaw at my heart?

If I do nothing, it will do something
I do not intend. How can I take
this attitude of annoyance and let it
turn to gratitude and grace? I pray
for a middle way. Yet well I know that
I will come upon this neutral zone
in a dark wood of waiting....

There the way is incubating.

I'm advocating the use of questions for yourself as well as for others, and not only as a method of creativity, but as a prayer practice to keep your own heart open. Being with others' physical hunger can cultivate in us a hunger for justice and spark our questioning why people suffer in a world of plenty (see Prayer Practice 15).

Practicing *Kenosis* in Relating to Others

Revisiting Keats's idea of negative capability recalls a major goal of honest to God prayer: to make us "capable of being in uncertainties, Mysteries, doubts, without an irritable reaching after fact & reason." Is that not what it means to live by grace?

Most of you reading this spend time with friends and colleagues who turn to you for wisdom in work, in families, in board meetings, in one-on-one and community settings. By learning to convert an insight into a thoughtful question, you may offer everyone several priceless gifts.

You slow down the rapid pace of conversation. While you're converting your insight into a question, you have to pause—a creative, prayerful space. When you give back another question to whomever you're with, it creates a second pause within that person. You've not only practiced *kenosis* for your own soul, but for the other's soul. You've given the gift of liminal spaces.

Playing around with moment-by-moment emptiness can free my ego from the need to act smart. Alan Alda of TV's *M*A*S*H* fame went on to host the PBS show *Scientific American Frontiers* for over ten years, interviewing renowned scientists. Speaking at Chautauqua Institution, New York, Alda told how when he tried to act smart by asking brilliant questions, it didn't work. The scientist would answer back with technical information, losing both the audience and Alda. He had to learn to ask dumb questions, in short, to practice negative capability. Experimenting with a "dumb question" frees me from needing to be the answer person by acting intelligent or by fixing my neighbor's problems.

In this spiritual tapestry, praying and playing with questions empowers others while creating a way to practice detachment to stay free to love. In T. S. Eliot's words, "Teach us to care and not to care."

PRACTICAL FRUITS OF *KENOSIS*

Although liminal spaces may thrust you into a temporary void of disorientation, the fruit of such experiences, if you follow through, is to return you to your passion and ground you in your life's purpose—which gives you a renewed focus and freedom. And that's the fruit of prayer, because you do not pray to be spiritual but to be free to love.

In a time of vocational emptiness, the metaphor of my life mission leapt off the page when I read it to a career counselor: "I am here on this earth to be a *link* between the Word and the world...." It keeps happening in big and little ways: I attend a social event and connect two persons who studied in Germany, or introduce a welder and a professor and they talk all evening; in spiritual companioning I meet with an evangelical Christian followed by someone for whom God died last year. In my writing, I link literature and life, religious themes of East and West, ancient wisdom and the latest world crisis, historical data and existential stories—and my soul comes alive. Zora Neale Hurston wrote in her classic book *Their Eyes Were Watching God*, "There are years of our lives that ask questions and years that answer."

PRACTICING DOING NOTHING

Regular practices of contemplative silence create empty spaces to make it more likely that you'll be awake when the sun rises—or when the sun sets. Sometimes the practices may seem heavy. You may drag your body to the place where you sit and meditate and doze off while you pray or put one aching leg over the other in yoga-like postures to keep your body supple. That's something like what I think C. S. Lewis meant by his book title *The Weight of Glory*. Every Olympic medalist or Carnegie Hall maestro understands the surprise gift of glory from weighty years of practice.

Four *Rs* for Relinquishing: Moving through Transitions

Cultivating mini-liminal spaces is a way of befriending the big transitions of personal or corporate loss and grief that take you by surprise. In his bestseller *Transitions*, William Bridges offers "strategies for coping with difficult, painful, and confusing times in your life." He says, "Things end, then you spend a time (or time-out) in the neutral zone, and then things begin anew." Bridges shows how this works not only for individuals but also for societies. I hope some of you experience contemplative ways of relating with family systems and faith communities in conflict: that amid difficult, painful, and confusing times, you create a prayerful neutral zone where things can begin anew.

> But how can you move through destructive experiences so they begin to metamorphose into life-giving gifts for yourself and your community?

But how can you move through destructive experiences so they begin to metamorphose into life-giving gifts for yourself and your community? People often give advice: "You should just let go!" Sometimes you want to scream, "But how?" In *Praying Our Goodbyes*, Joyce Rupp outlines four continuing stages on the road to healthy relinquishment and new life.

Recognition of the loss or change and unresolved fear beneath it is the beginning step. Only by being aware and by naming the "demons" can they be offered to become what the Greeks called the *daemon*—a source of creative energy.

Reflection means meditating, praying—or playing with grief "like a child's toy" as the Russian writer Maxim Gorky put it. Playing with words in a journal, poem-making, walking with the loss or change or talking it out opens the heart's eyes to see potential gain in the pain, which may also be aspects of spiritual direction.

Ritualizing means engaging in repetitive spiritual practices—physical, verbal and visual, musical—to notice gifts in the shifts of change and loss: a symbolic object of nature, a chant, a morning walk, centering prayer, tai chi or exercises where you breathe in and hold, then breathe out and release.

Reorienting literally means turning east again, to the orient, the sunrise where new insights dawn. Any practices that help rejuvenate the resilient child in you will bear the fruit of compassion and courage to enter the dark tunnel of transition with hope.[1]

I view all four *r* words under the umbrella of the big *R*: relinquishment. Over time, such practices can provide the *how* for relinquishing, so that our lives can be reoriented, re-Eastered. Yet we don't reach the new orientation without struggles.

Practicing Relinquishment: Two Forms

In my experience, there are two main forms of relinquishment. You have experiences where at a point in time you're able to relinquish hurts or hopes. Other times, as with intense addictions and traumatic losses, you practice what I call a "twelve-step," day-by-day process of relinquishing. Either form can lead to reorientation.

POINT-IN-TIME RELINQUISHMENT

In 1978 I gave up on a dream and yielded to circumstances of necessity when I slammed an ordinary file drawer shut—a kind of prayer unawares. My wife and I had applied to adopt a son from Korea. During the process, we moved from south central Pennsylvania to the Philadelphia area in a different county. We had to redo the paperwork with a new social worker; things slowed down.

Nearly two years into this process, on a hot June day, we got a letter from the national agency saying the parent agency in Korea and its American counterpart were having problems; there were no prospects for a child and we could write to another agency—list enclosed.

I recall after my wife and I read the letter and talked of our changed circumstances (our recent move and the traumatic death of a beloved aunt), I stuffed the letter into a folder. Then I slammed the file drawer shut—letting go of some anger—probably with an under-the-breath exclamation. As I look back on it now, that was a prayer of relinquishment. We seemed to put the issue out of our minds.

That September, I was on a staff retreat in a neighboring church's carriage house, when the wall phone began to ring and ring. Annoyed, finally I decided to answer. It was my wife, Freddy, saying, "We have a son!" I cannot describe our instant euphoria: we had both literally died to the dream of ever having a son—who's now in his thirties and recently married. When our four-year-old joy boy arrived at New York's Kennedy Airport at Christmastime that year, he was pure gift.

You know the story: you release the bird and if it doesn't return, it wasn't really yours; if it returns it's total gift. However, I believe such one-time relinquishments are rare.

DAY-AT-A-TIME RELINQUISHING

The second form involves an experience of a continuous, day-at-a-time process of relinquishing. Life may deal you a wound that's so daily present that there won't be a once-and-forever relinquishment: traumatic injury, chronic disability, vocational crisis, suicide, tragic death or disappearance. You learn to practice repeated "twelve-step" relinquishing.

Sometimes there can be no closure. A person suddenly dies or disappears. That is when rituals can help. You may write an unsent letter, burn a letter, converse with a person not present using an empty chair, name the gifts from a negative relationship, or meditate on an object of nature that symbolizes your feelings. Write your way through the pain, using a dialogue in your journal. Act it out; dance with it; do physical exercise, tai chi, or yoga. Choreograph a gesture. Talk it out with a confidant. Release it with a repeated breath prayer. All of these activities aid in the work of day-to-day relinquishment.

At age forty-five such a crisis occurred for me through a painful church conflict, resulting in my leaving as pastor of a large congregation where I had expected to retire. During a transitional period, I served as a chaplain and began training in spiritual guidance and retreat work at Shalem Institute in Washington, DC.

The emptiness I felt in leaving parish ministry led to my gathering a small Clearness Committee to discern my sense of call (see Prayer Practice 16). I shared my initial ripples of finding and founding an "oasis" in the desert of this aloneness. In Quaker fashion, people I had invited then asked me open questions. Sometime later, I gathered a board and we founded Oasis Ministries for Spiritual Development, a not-for-profit organization to offer retreats and spiritual formation training (see www.oasismin.org).

Still in the pit of my stomach I carried the void of not writing sermons and bearing a word of hope within a community week by week. So I started to write about spiritual disciplines, first for myself. Then I began to believe I had a message for other burned-out leaders and seekers. I began to pray my life mission: that God would *link* my writings with a publisher and *link* my passion for spiritual practices with people who needed renewal.

At the same time I knew I needed to detach from making these burgeoning spiritual ministries and writings my "show." Once I was responsible for a major conference, when the announced nationally known speaker became ill for several months. While driving from Harrisburg to Lancaster, Pennsylvania, on Interstate I-283, a prayer of the heart emerged that seated itself in my breathing: *Lord link....* *I relinquish....* First it was to link the speaker ... and relinquish; then it was to link participants to attend; the morning of the conference it was to link the crackling microphone!

Over the decades since then, I have used the ritual of this (or another) repeated breath prayer (*Lord link.... I relinquish....*) to detach from my pet ideas or past obsessions. Sometimes the thing I'm praying about happens, sometimes not, but always I aim to remain free to love. Instead of "answered" prayers, I call my current concerns "answering" prayers as I jot them on sticky notes in my journal—because prayer is an ongoing process, not a mechanical technique.

Naming Issues, Reflecting, and Creating Rituals for Detachment

The way toward genuine relinquishment is to recognize, reflect on, and ritualize weighty life issues so that your soul gets reoriented. Depending on your personality and spiritual temperament, some methods for prayer become more meaningful than others.

In my Denver neighborhood I've discovered two kinds of oak trees. One loses its leaves after frost in the fall, but the other loses its leaves only in the spring as the new growth begins. Perhaps it's a parable of timing in the process of relinquishing, but in either case we need to shed our attachment to the old before new life can come.

RELEASING EMOTIONAL BAGGAGE

As I meet with people and listen, they tell me how hard it is to let go of unresolved anger, resentment, guilt, grief, or feelings of being controlled or misunderstood. Sometimes I say: Pause ... now allow a word or phrase, or an image or metaphor, to come to mind that encapsulates how the Spirit is inviting you ... to find what you need to name and claim to be more whole. If what emerges is a word or a phrase ("peace ... release ..."), repeat it as your unique breath prayer or centering prayer, to relinquish the concern as often as it surfaces in your mind; if it's an image or metaphor ("clear glass"), visualize it as it surfaces (see Prayer Practice 2).

Other times I use a focusing exercise with physical gestures. I invite a person to pause ... to focus on where in their body the feeling they describe seems to lodge ... to be with that sensation ... then gently place their hands on that area of the body... and next to imagine relinquishing the tension by exhaling several times while creating a gesture of releasing ... finally to return their hands in a gesture of healing or integrating (see Prayer Practice 17).

If it seems appropriate, I may put on the Beatles' CD *Let It Be* and allow the words and images to waft over the tensions in the person's soul (see Prayer Practice 18). Once, for a young Italian man, the word *adagio* ("slowly" or "at ease") emerged as his centering prayer word; later I played a CD of multiple versions of Samuel Barber's "Adagio." Or I may reach for pastels and paper and suggest the person "art" the issue they've been using words to describe; or I place a lump of clay in a person's hands and suggest they see how the clay wants to shape itself. Each of these exercises, of course, makes use of silent spaces before, during, and after any such experiential exercise.

> Prayer is an ongoing process, not a mechanical technique.

EXORCISING THE DEMON OF PERFECTIONISM

Part of the process of relinquishment means shedding our attachment to wanting to look perfect, trying to get things right. It's the demon at the heart of micromanaging and political cover-ups. In Western cultures we tend to operate out of an all-or-nothing mindset. Go on a diet. Start an exercise routine. Commit to spiritual practices. A year later: it didn't work.

I once complained to my orthopedic doctor that the back exercises he prescribed did more harm than good. "I do them for a week; then my back is sorer and I have to quit for two weeks."

"Two things," he said. "First, be gentle on yourself. Exercise until you stretch the muscles, but not until you feel intense pain. Second, aim for four days out of seven. If you slip back to three days, just move your inner computer cursor in the right direction."

What I now practice for my back, I offer as sound counsel for any physical, mental, and spiritual discipline. I use a phrase: *Never obligation, only invitation.* When I can't take my normal walk in the mornings, I take a miniwalk to keep the pattern going. When I can't take twenty minutes for centering prayer, I take two minutes.

This is about *honest* praying. "Saints are not perfect humans. But in their own individual fashion they become *authentic* human beings, endowed with the capacity to awaken that vocation in others," writes Robert Ellsberg in *All Saints.* You may know this in your head, but have trouble letting it get to your heart.

The hands can create a good route to the heart. I find grace in the grit of working with Habitat for Humanity. Part of me will know I need to spend a precious Saturday writing, but another part knows the break of engaging in kinesthetic service will be good for my soul and for the writing. While writing this book, another project just won out again, and I found myself still "writing" while rehabbing old handrails.

As volunteers go and come, each leaving our less-than-perfect doorjambs and baseboards, it creates a funny sort of therapy. A perfectionist would walk off the job at 9 a.m. I've come to see it's worth several visits to a psychiatrist to cure my perfectionism. Constructing genuine community means building on each other's less-than-perfect efforts. My psyche gets healed a bit when I surround myself with fallible humans on behalf of humanity.

RELINQUISHING RELIGIOUS PERFECTIONIST LANGUAGE

Religious language can reinforce a do-it-right-or-don't-do-it-at-all attitude. Most folks today mentally translate perfection as perfectionism, and perfect as *faultless.* Yet both the original biblical Greek *telios,* and the Latin *perfectum* (behind our English word), mean "complete, mature, or whole." And the noun *telos* means "goal or finish line." One way I script my own psyche is to say, "That's ideal!"—instead of perfect—when I finish a project.

Jesus does not say, "Be perfect...." but rather, "Become complete, therefore, as your Abba in heaven is complete" (Matthew 5:48, AT). Luke's Gospel has already helped by translating the phrase, "Be compassionate as your Abba is compassionate" (6:36, AT)—and be compassionate (or merciful) to your self.

Our culture inflicts this damning perfectionism on us. A family with a member in recovery from anorexia can witness to the subtle, crippling effects of a Barbie doll perfection syndrome and exercise addiction. The apostle Paul can say, "Not that I have already obtained this or have already reached the goal (*telos*); but I press on to make it my own, because Christ Jesus has made me his own.... Let those of us then who are mature (*telioi*) be of the same mind" (Philippians 3:12, 15).

TRANSFORMING PERFECTIONIST SELF-TALK

I notice that I find myself saying, "I *should* do such and such." Self-talk affects our unconscious thinking and acting. Decades ago I remember reading psychologist Karen Horney's phrase "the tyranny of the should," which is only slightly more philosophical than the *Saturday Night Live* line, "You're shoulding on yourself!" When I catch myself saying "I should" do a certain task, if I can translate it "I'd like to...." or "I need to...." then it lies close to my passion. I move from "should" to "can" to "will"—then discern when and how to act on it. If a task seems only like a should, I find a way to relinquish it—sometimes by supporting someone who has a passion for it. Never obligation, only invitation: language shapes attitude and action.

SABBATH TIME: AN RX FOR PERFECTIONISM

Some day needs to be a "sabbath"—one day out of seven to empty our task-driven agendas. Practicing sabbath and pausing for mini-sabbaths can act as an Rx for perfectionism, a way of trusting the universe of divine Love to provide for what needs to be done on other days, or by other ways, or by other folks. To fast from my workaholic tendencies by celebrating with others and God is to claim my humanity and free myself from the demon of "it's all about me."

The need to control people and situations is one of the demonic expressions of perfectionism. At the root of the demon of micromanaging lies a secret fear of shame: *I don't want another's half-botched job to reflect poorly on my project.* Detachment means learning to trust God by trusting people. It means loving God for the world's sake, losing self to find your real Self.

Humility, in a strange way, is actually spiritual self-confidence: confidence that you can celebrate the gifts of others, rather than belittle them, while at the same time claiming your own. It's a God-confidence that there are enough gifts for both your neighbor and you to claim your potential for the good of the cosmos, without exploiting or belittling each other. And that's a good definition of *telios*: mature, complete.

Practices for Cultivating Relinquishment

Emptiness as Space for God

I invite you to become aware of some emptiness in your life: an unfulfilled desire you may rarely express. Gently get in touch with it. One somewhat private person said, "It's that my mother died and never got to see my husband and children. I think of it often." It may be a kind of a spiritual homing instinct, "a God-shaped vacuum." Once you name it, gently look at ways you may be using to fill it—some good, some not so good. Prayerfully begin to offer the emptiness by thinking of it as "space for God." Ask: What's the invitation in the emptiness?

An Examen of Liminal Spaces

What are the "front porches" or the "back porches" of the house of your life? What are the doorways of your life? What title would you give the doorway to your childhood? What would you name the threshold from childhood to adolescence? From adolescence to young adulthood? To adulthood? More important, I invite you now to ask: What threshold are you entering now? What title would you give to the doorway for this chapter of your life?

Table Blessing from Latin America

O God, to those who have hunger give bread,
and to those who have bread give a hunger for justice.*

*Explain justice as fairness if used with younger children.

The Clearness Committee

The Clearness Committee (originally developed by Quakers to discern readiness for marriage) is a helpful tool for individuals facing a variety of vocational issues. Normally the "focus person," the one seeking clearness, enlists five or six trusted persons (although someone else may suggest the idea) from various contexts of his or her life. The focus person writes up his or her situation in advance and circulates it to the group, asking one to serve as convener, another as note taker. (Allow two hours for the meeting.) The convener opens the meeting with silence, then asks the focus person to give a fresh statement of the concern. The convener calls for silence again, then invites discerning questions ("How did that experience guide you?") and observations ("I'm hearing four possible careers....")—but not "fix-it" advice ("Why don't you…?"). All happens in a meditative atmosphere. The group may end with a spoken or physical blessing (such as prayerfully laying hands on the focus person in silence). The group may be reconvened.[2]

Option: You may include your life mission statement, night dreams, daydreams, and stories in your notes for a Clearness Committee.

Prayer Practice 17

A Focusing Exercise in Three Gestures

You may begin with a simple prayer or a chant. Now I invite you to close your eyes and get in touch with some area of stress or tension in your life: physical, relational, personal, or institutional (take a few minutes). Simply be with that tension or stress, not censoring it, just noticing it. Begin to focus on where in your body you sense the tension most (head, neck, shoulders, heart, stomach, groin, thighs, legs, feet, or elsewhere). Take a few moments of silence just to be with it gently in God's presence. [3]

1. Now see if you might place your hand or hands on that area of stress or angst; or you may place your two hands on slightly different areas. Again, the goal is just to be with that stress or tension, breathing slowly (a few minutes).
2. Find a second gesture … one of releasing the stress or tension … offering this area of angst to God, with several deep, slow, exhaled breaths (a few more minutes).
3. Allow a third gesture to emerge with your hands, this time one of healing … or one of integration … or of invitation … (a few minutes longer).

If you used a prayer or a chant at the beginning, softly begin to pray or sing again….

Process: Take time to make a few notes in your journal.

Idea: Converse about your experience with a trusted spiritual friend, in person or by phone.

Option (for a group): Before leading the exercise, create safe space by turning chairs (widely spaced) in a semicircle facing outward to windows or walls.

Prayer Practice 18

"Let It Be"

Listen to the Beatles' song "Let It Be" (on mp3 or the CD *Let It Be*). "Mother Mary" refers to Paul McCartney's dream of his mother, who died when he was fourteen. The title also might be heard as a subtle take on Mary's response when the angel Gabriel announced she would bear a child: "Let it be to me according to your word" (Luke 1:38). As you hear the words "let it be," or repeat them in your mind, imagine letting go of an issue that you can't control, or accepting a challenge that may want to birth itself in you.

Prayer as Paradox

Integrating

CHAPTER SEVEN

Rediscovering Mystery

The Grounding for Paradox

Life is not a problem to be solved, but a mystery to be lived.
—GABRIEL MARCEL

I have integrated all my diversity, and I have individualized all my wholeness.
—HADEWIJCH, *THE COMPLETE WORKS*

Beyond rational and critical thinking, we need to be called again. This can lead to the discovery of a "second naiveté," which is a return to the joy of our first naiveté, but now totally new, inclusive, and mature thinking.
—PAUL RICOEUR

*B*oth/and *prayer integrates the creative divine Mystery in an either/or world that wants you to choose between seeming contradictions: productive vs. contemplative, instant have-it-now vs. consistent growing-into. Genuine prayer becomes countercultural and paradoxical: finding* stillness while in motion; being alone yet all one; turning inward while turning outward; empowering the real Self while relinquishing the false self. Yet relinquishing does not mean rejecting, but rather integrating your shadow side, even finding treasure in it. Out of the rubbish you discard, there grows new life.

This is the night of life and its direction is the North, when humanly you can hardly see, but on a primal spiritual level, like the owl, you see more clearly. Like the god Janus, you face inward and outward at once. At night you can focus on the depth of the universe and, paradoxically, on death as a doorway to life. The night that may have seemed fearful becomes the beautiful night of lovers and poets, or spiritually, the soul's dark night.

Integrative vs. Eclectic: The Core of Paradox

Integrity is a lifelong fruit of a day-by-day process of integrating your life with your experience of God.

"All of us here are pretty much eclectic," a speaker said, alluding to varied spiritual traditions. But in that moment, I thought, *No, not eclectic—integrative!* At break time I was conversing with another participant who had the same thought. "How do they sound different?" we asked each other.

I've since raised the question with friends over dinner, strangers at airports, and companions in spiritual direction. Recently, one said to me, "Well, eclectic sounds like dabbling, grabbing a little bit from here and there to see what works, what feels good. Integrative sounds more genuine." Another said, "Eclectic seems like drawing from the surface; integrative connects with the core of who you are." Others play with related words: the process of *integrating* leads to the goal of *integrity*.

INTEGRITY AND MYSTERY

Rather than compartmentalizing actions and intentions, integrity means incorporating spiritual values and practices into the whole of life.

Integrity is not a thing you grab and put in your pocket. It's about living into the transforming Mystery while simultaneously turning to Reality.

A person of integrity is one who practices a continual habit of discernment. When confronted with an unexpected choice, a person of integrity asks, which decision aligns best with who I am? Which choice would be more true to the core of my own soul, to my life experience and my experience of God? "This above all: to thine own self be true" (Shakespeare, *Hamlet*).

> Integrity is not a thing you grab and put in your pocket. It's about living into the transforming Mystery while simultaneously turning to Reality.

This kind of integrative prayer restores a second naiveté: now you can reclaim religious language beyond a literal level, as a metaphor of the deeper Mystery.[1] You can live creatively balancing a tension of opposites.

NARROWING THE GAP

But isn't all genuine praying paradoxical? From your first awareness, you discover that reality is bittersweet, with flecks of grace in the grit. In the rhythm of empowerment and relinquishment, like breathing, you experience the paradox of inspiration and expiration—life and death. You've seen inklings of this union of opposites all along.

Why then this theme of prayer as paradox? Because the more you become aware and practice the Tao of these rhythms, the gap between the poles begins to narrow, until you come home in the very moment of dissonance.

Early one summer morning, I leaped from the front porch at Chautauqua, New York, eager to grab my bicycle and get to the Episcopal chapel on time. But my bike was gone! Immediately, I thought, *Aargh, my son borrowed it and left it somewhere.* I turned, and in that instant, I recalled that *I* had ridden it to a lecture hall the night before, become intrigued with the presentation, and walked back with the speaker, leaving my bike behind.

I've reflected how I might have held onto my conjured-up resentment toward my son and done damage for an hour, or all day, or even longer. The gift of honest to God prayer is that the gap begins to narrow between the moment of angst and the moment of awareness—becoming prayer as paradox.

Dancing with Paradox: Integrating Mystery

Prayer as paradox becomes a dance that returns you to your wildest dreams, but now with spiritual detachment. Paradox is our Western concept like the Chinese Tao and the Eastern sense of mystery. Some Christians flinch at mystery, yet Jesus spoke of the mystery of the realm of God and Paul called Christ the mystery. Prayer as paradox is no mere flip-flopping from one extreme to another, like Dr. Jekyll and Mr. Hyde, but rather integrating conflicting aspects within your self, God, and others.

"I have integrated all my diversity, and I have individualized all my wholeness," writes the thirteenth-century Flemish mystic Hadewijch. Where can you find a more profound yet practical witness to genuine integrity?

Integrating moves beyond merely tolerating differences; entering into mystery means embracing contradictions to create a "third way." Like a dance, you step forward and backward in a unity of stillness and motion. In T. S. Eliot's words, "at the still point, there the dance is." Here we explore dimensions of the Mystery.

DANCING WITH COMMUNITY AND SOLITUDE

Without the practice of community, solitude degenerates into isolation and self-absorption; without the practice of solitude, community degenerates into enmeshment and codependency.

Everyone needs time alone in solitude in order to be all one in community. Healthy community (even between two lovers) needs the compassionate discipline of allowing each other space to nurture the self alone, and then coming together to celebrate their unique experiences. Without the intentional rhythm of aloneness, any community will be fragmented; its members will not be all one; they will not be intimate—even if two physical bodies intertwine in sex.

At times of being alone, you can feel all one. We all breathe the same air. When you've been alone physically, have you ever experienced being in closer communion with someone who's an ocean away than with a person next to you at lunch? Practicing intentional prayer in solitude promotes unity with all.

Conversely, a New Jersey woman gave me a new slant on solitude, among others' glowing stories of solitary joys and blessings. "I have a funny idea about the discipline of solitude," she said. "Every group I'm a part of, it seems I'll be the odd person out, different in my thinking. It gets lonely. Yet I'll hang in there, because I feel a passion to let my voice be heard." In a group of social activists, she feels like the lone voice advocating prayer; in a prayer group, she feels like the lone voice for justice. She embraces her solitude to live in solidarity with all.

I recall getting surprised at the end of our first year of "Spiritual Direction for Spiritual Guides," Oasis Ministries' training program in contemplative prayer and spiritual

> We cannot survive this human brokenness for long without like-minded soul friends—*anam cara*, as the Irish call it.

direction. We had assumed these folks, who enrolled and traveled distances each month, came for the solitude and personal spiritual growth. But the year-end evaluations revealed the number one priority was safe community—bonding with like-minded individuals who shared the joy of solitude and prayer with a passion for justice.

Personal spirituality needs the messy membrane of community to be complete. We cannot survive this human brokenness for long without like-minded soul friends—*anam cara*, as the Irish call it. If you live

with your spiritual eyes awake, you never know when a solitary individual will reveal the tip of their submerged iceberg, if you or I seem
like a "safe person." Then you have found the seed of community.

DANCING WITH THE OUTWARD AND THE INWARD

Because contemplative spirituality seems more natural for introverts,
I feel a special passion, as an extrovert, to interpret prayer for active
people for whom introspection is not so natural. Sometimes the *via
positiva* leads to the *via negativa,* active to contemplative, in what I call
extroverted mysticism, as in this poem by William Butler Yeats.

> My fiftieth year had come and gone.
> I sat, a solitary man,
> In a crowded London shop,
> An open book and empty cup
> On the marble table-top.
>
> While on the shop and street I gazed
> My body of a sudden blazed;
> And twenty minutes more or less,
> It seemed, so great my happiness
> That I was blessèd and could bless.[2]

While meditating on the bustling shop and street, the inward reverie of
contemplation took Yeats into a deep prayer of contemplative gratitude.
In a similar way, when a student went on a cross-cultural trip from the
U.S. to Cuba, he and his lover each made a pact to keep a personal journal. His outward journey sparked their unique inward journeys.

But the inward can also ignite the outward. As an ordinary school-
teacher in the 1970s, Julia Esquivel had no plans ever to be known as
a political activist and a feminist theologian. In personal conversation,
she told me how she had begun to have disturbing mystical visions
about her beloved Guatemala. When she began to express these in

revolutionary poetry, the government silenced her, forcing her to live exiled in Europe. Now back in Guatemala, Esquivel exemplifies how embracing fear can in the same moment mean embracing faith, wedding mystical experience and risk-taking action.

In walking a labyrinth, you participate in this unifying rhythm as you journey inward, leaving the world of action, pausing in the still center. Then you journey outward, returning to the world. To find a labyrinth near you, see www.labyrinthlocator.com.

DANCING WITH THE FEAR AND THE GIFT

In *The Good Life*, Harvard's late chaplain Peter Gomes tells an amazing story of cellist Yo-Yo Ma in his early years auditioning with the Russian-born master Mstislav Rostropovich. At several points, as Rostropovich interrupted and gesticulated wildly, it was impossible to know whether he was angry or pleased with Ma. At the end, the elder master hugged the youthful performer and showered him with kisses. Among audience cheers, a translator bellowed that never had the maestro been in the presence of such genius. Yet Ma says he still experiences fear using the gift of doing what he passionately loves.

In my thirties I presented a paper at Duquesne University in Pittsburgh for a regional meeting of the Society of Biblical Literature. In late afternoon the presider introduced me, the last presenter: "And now the paper we've all been waiting for, 'Bultmann, Pannenberg, and Kunta Kinte.'" (I would connect Alex Haley's ancestor Kunta's suffering in the hold of the slave ship as told in *Roots* with Jesus's passion.) Such fear gripped me that I trembled. Knowing nothing in those days of breath prayers, I never recovered, even during the question and answer session. I felt so shamed that I never again presented to such a group, though now I lecture at seminaries.

Two decades later, Nancy Bieber, a staff member with Oasis Ministries, was presenting: "We are called the Society of Friends, but also Quakers—which comes from the fact that when a Friend rises to speak, he or she may 'quake,' a sign that one is speaking a truth greater than oneself." In that moment, her simple comment transformed a smoldering inner wound into an empowering revelation. I had trembled in awe of a truth greater than myself.

Are such stories not analogies of our relationship to Life—to God? It's impossible to tell in some experiences that we are being affirmed and loved when we, out of fear, misperceive it as rejection. Living vitally can be like playing roughhouse with the Love at the heart of universe—a Love Supreme longing to affirm and bless us.

> Living vitally can be like playing roughhouse with the Love at the heart of universe—a Love Supreme longing to affirm and bless us.

DANCING WITH SOUNDS AND SILENCE

The paradox of genuine prayer is marked by the healthy integration of silence and sounds, like the configuration of darks and lights in a classic painting. Kōans or riddles abound with metaphors of speech in silence in primal texts like the *Tao Te Ching*: "The word that can be spoken / is not the eternal Word." In Jewish Christian scriptures we also find such kōans, as in Psalm 19:2:

> Day to day pours forth speech,
> and night to night declares knowledge.
> There is no speech, nor are there words;
> their voice is not heard;
> yet their voice goes out through all the earth,
> and their words to the end of the world.

Such wordless words in creation call us back to the truth that deeds speak louder than words. Much of the Hebrew Bible and the Gospel sayings of Jesus are far more akin to Eastern kōans than to Western logical and theological concepts. Jesus says, "To you has been given the secret—or mystery [*mysterion* in Greek] of the kingdom of God, but for those outside, everything comes in parables" (Mark 4:11). It's Emily Dickinson again, telling truth but telling it "slant."

Ivan Illich, who trained educators in linguistic and intercultural awareness, writes, "It takes more time and effort and delicacy to learn the silence of a people than to learn its sounds.... The learning of the grammar of silence is an art much more difficult to learn than the grammar of sounds." A Pueblo friend tells me it's the same in her Native culture: listen for the truth by attending to the silences.

In a noisy world, spending time praying in honest to God silence is a paradoxical and profound way to practice listening with your neighbor. "Right speech comes out of silence, and right silence comes out of speech," writes theologian Dietrich Bonhoeffer in *Life Together*. While on retreat in a noisy city in India, my guide gave me a method for paradoxically finding silence amid the noise (see Prayer Practice 19).

DANCING WITH THE CHILD AND THE ELDER

It's spiritually transforming to discover what's playful in the serious thing, and the serious thing in what's playful. Sometimes adults need to discipline themselves *not* to work in order to return to play and get lost again in wonder. Without stepping back to wonder, the best methods in business, medicine, parenting, politics, or spirituality become a drag or, worse yet, destroy the very thing we think we're accomplishing.

In 1971, China was sealed off from the world. No one would have predicted that the U.S.-China Ping-Pong match would be the key to opening a country with eight and a half million people to Western nations. Headlining the event as "The Ping Heard Round the World," *Time* magazine hailed the players as the world's most improbable—and most naive—group of diplomats. Probably never had a sport become such an effective tool of international diplomacy.

Here's paradox again: creative breakthroughs wed advanced theories of politics, or science, or theology with youthful wonder and play. Awareness begins with restoring the healthy child and leads to playful projects for serious purposes. We can never go beyond awareness, only deepen it into mystery.

In May 1955, ten-year-old Ronald awakened in the night in his Bronx home to find his father dead of a sudden heart attack at age thirty-three. A year later, reading a Classics Illustrated comic version of H. G. Wells's *The Time Machine*, the boy knew at once what he had to do: build a time machine to go back and be with his TV-repairman father again to discover the mysteries of light. So the University of Connecticut physics professor Ronald Mallett's fantasy of bringing his father back to life spawned his lifelong career as a leader in time-travel research, taking Einstein's general theory of relativity to quantum levels. In his book and its Spike Lee movie version, *Time Traveler*, Mallett tells how his childhood fantasy led to his serious lifelong science vocation.

DANCING WITH PRIMAL AND MODERN

Mystery lets you reclaim the creative child at a deeper level: a second naiveté. In the first naiveté, many of us start out mouthing religious language and thinking of God as a kind of divine puppeteer somewhere up there or out there in the cosmos.

Then, in a slow or sudden crisis, that childish image of God gets shattered. As Moses, in anger, shatters the tablets of the Ten Commandments, so the same Hebrew word (*shabar*) is used to describe an infant who shatters the womb in childbirth (Exodus 32:19; Isaiah 37:3). In the shattering, the tapestry of paradox is deconstructed before it can be reconstructed. You relinquish the womb-like security of fixed religious dogmas and enter that period of emptiness, a liminal state, a cloud of unknowing. Enter the "postmodern" spiritual journey—one that lacks fixed points for orientation.

The "modern" part means using your reason: the naive three-story universe no longer works; you can't stomach a God that created everything in six literal twenty-four-hour days or punishes people with natural disasters. You realize the ancients used myth and metaphor to interpret reality; you believe in evolution and understand scientific explanations for earthquakes and tsunamis.

But you also know enough about subatomic physics that some things go beyond reason: physicists say you can know how fast something's moving or where it is; that is, you can know its motion or its position—but not both. But light just goes ahead with both: it's a wave and a particle at once. That's the "post" modern part of you that believes in mystery that goes beyond reason.

Maybe I was already a bit postmodern back in 1957 when the Soviet Russians came back from orbiting the first spaceship, Sputnik. They announced they had not found God, but I was not upset; it had never occurred to me that God was up there or out there.

Yet postmodern folks go right on using the language of "up" and "down"—the second naiveté. We return to childhood terms, but use them metaphorically, not literally. The computer is down—it's not operational. "Downsizing" a corporation does not mean shrinking its building.

Aren't we still modern? Don't we use reason *and* technology? We can be primal *and* modern. So I propose a new term: primodern. Metaphors allow us to be grown-up and naive at the same time.

I tell a spiritual companion in California that I will "walk" with him through a major life transition, but I do not mean I will develop huge legs that straddle all the way from Denver to San Diego (we meet via the Internet). In the same way I can say God has "walked" with me through many dangers, toils, and snares. It is a very personal walk, but God does not need feet and toes.

I'm calling for a new kind of spirituality, open to questioning yet passionate with love. Primodern spirituality integrates our primal yearnings with our modern learnings. It's a call to integrate critical thinking with contemplative living. We can use critical reasoning to deconstruct ancient tales to discover what happened, while also returning to myth and metaphor to discover what still happens. Aren't there times when you can still see a burning bush or even walk on water?

DANCING WITH STILLNESS AND MOTION

"One who sees the inaction that is in action and the action that is in in-action is wise indeed. Even when engaged in action, that one remains poised in the tranquility of the Atman," says the Hindu Bhagavad-Gita.[3] Let me relate this text with my experience.

In the arched window of the "sabbath room," where I meet with folks for spiritual companioning, hangs a circular stained-glass por-trayal of a boat being tossed on stormy aqua waves, with a cobalt-blue sky and a tiny orange crescent encircling the boat's sails. For me it represents the Gospel version of this Hindu saying. I imagine Jesus—asleep on the storm-tossed boat, yet poised in tranquility when terri-fied disciples wake him—as he says, "'Peace! Be still!' And there was a dead calm" (Mark 4:39). A sacred text changes from back then to a here-and-now experience, as I wake the "sleeping Christ" in my heart in times of crisis.

To be still, that is not difficult. But to achieve stillness while in motion, that is the miracle! In a surprise moment when someone meeting with me pauses and discovers the still point of peace in a fearful place, we have reclaimed the "miracle" language in a life-giving way. We learn, as T. S. Eliot puts it, to "be still and still moving" on this journey into a deepening union with everything we thought was separated. Action happens in contemplation, stillness while in motion.

DANCING WITH ACCUSATION AND AFFIRMATION

Ironically, psalm-like anger at the absence of God may be a way of affirming divine presence. I'm writing this during what Christians call "Holy Week," starting with Jesus's triumphant celebration on Sunday and climaxing with the crucifixion on Friday. The earliest Gospel, Mark, reports only one saying of Jesus from the cross (from Psalm 22:1), "My God, my God, why have you forsaken me?" Here Jesus's honest to God praying gives voice to raw human angst, even accusation—*Why?*—in the face of unexplained suffering and political violence.

In *The Town Beyond the Wall*, Elie Wiesel, whose suffering in the Holocaust gives him more right than most of us to accuse God, places on the lips of one of his most rebellious characters these anguished and yet strangely hopeful words: "I want to blaspheme, and I can't quite manage it. I go up against [God], I shake my fist, I froth with rage, but it's still a way of telling Him that He's there, that He exists, that He's never the same twice, that denial itself is an offering to His grandeur. The shout becomes a prayer in spite of me."[4]

> Aren't there times when you can still see a burning bush or even walk on water?

To care enough to be angry is already a hint of divine stirrings in your angst. The ultimate insult to another is to ignore their presence, to refuse any response, even in the face of indignity. At least the in-your-face atheism of Richard Dawkins's *The God Delusion* and Christopher Hitchens's *God Is Not Great: How Religion Poisons Everything* has revived talk about God.

A woman told me of endless sufferings: childhood abuse, domestic violence, manipulative religion, betrayed relationships, then the tragic death of her one genuine lover. She had become numb, she said, anesthetized by apathy. Then one day when she came home, she noticed a little wilted flower near her sidewalk. As she entered her kitchen to get water for it, she began to cry. "I realized I could still care," she said. "A tiny wilted plant created a pinhole to know that divine Love was still there." A spark of caring, even if masked in anger or apathy, can ignite a slow fuse of praying into the Mystery.

DANCING WITH THE LIGHT IN THE DARK

The essence of prayer as paradox is the classic dark night of the soul, which creates a deepening trust in God, yet simultaneously an absence of the felt Presence. You may experience darkness all around, yet trust the Mystery. "Even the darkness is not dark to you; the night is as bright as the day, for darkness is as light to you" (Psalm 139:12).

Prophetic wisdom teaches, "I will give you the treasures of darkness" (Isaiah 45:3). Thus the mystery of Love can transform destructive darkness into a night of beauty. Prayer becomes dancing in the dark.

Dark speaks of destruction, disaster, death, disintegration. *Night* conveys newness, nearness, intimacy, transformation. Taken together a *dark night* experience can transform harsh diminishments into a thing of depth and beauty. It has a long history.

"Moses entered the thick darkness where God was," says the Hebrew Bible (Exodus 20:21). Psalms portray God as present, though often absent: "Why do you hide your face?" (43:24). Nicodemus came to see Jesus by night, when Jesus told him, "You must be born anew" (John 3:3, AT). The apostle Paul, after encountering Christ, retreated at once to Arabia and Syria for a three-year blackout period before contacting the establishment church in Jerusalem (see Galatians 1:15–18). Plotinus, Denys, and Gregory of Nyssa in the early church spoke of the abyss of God's love as a "dark ray"—which we now know scientifically as black light.

Like the apostle Paul, Abu Hamid al-Ghazali, a prominent Muslim scientist and theologian, underwent a spiritual breakdown in the late eleventh century: "I have poked into every dark recess, I have made an assault on every problem, I have plunged into every abyss.... God shriveled my tongue...."[5] Al-Ghazali left his professorship in Baghdad to retreat for several years. Renewed by Sufi practices, he returned as a great Sufi voice for uniting reason *and* mystical experience.

The dark night is especially linked with the fifteenth-century Spanish mystic John of the Cross, whose childhood poverty contained a seed of his suffering and genius. Young John worked in a hospital and went to school by day. He would study late into the night. Thus as a youth John had already made night his friend. So, when imprisoned as an adult, John could write in his classic poem, "O guiding night! O night more lovely than the dawn!"

At times the soul's night can arrive unbidden, with no outward crisis, as an evolution of your spiritual journey. Other times it's precipitated by outward circumstances such as a physical, emotional, relational, or vocational breakup. In either case, the key to transformation is learning to respond rather than react to life's surprises, in a way that blesses the world and your own soul.

Light Beams

> Great Spirit:
> hold us all ways in your sway,
> help us ever more to stay
> in your rays of light,
> in your gaze at night,
> in your ways of right.
>
> Let your fiery rays converge
> and merge to set ablaze
> the tender tinder of our hearts,
> and there ignite a living flame of love
> that shall surely guide us
> better than a known way:
> that shall surely guide us
> better than a known way,
> better than a known way,
> better than a known way.

CHAPTER EIGHT

The Active Contemplative Life

The Process of Paradox

Now I become myself. It's taken
Time, many years and places;
I have been dissolved and shaken,
Worn other people's faces.
—MAY SARTON, *COLLECTED POEMS, 1930-1993*

Faith is the bird that feels the light and sings when the
dawn is still dark.
—RABINDRANATH TAGORE

The presence of the star does not excuse us from the
difficult territory through which it is guiding us.
—DAVID WHYTE, *CROSSING THE UNKNOWN SEA*

*T**he process of praying as paradox is not to achieve balance, but rather to learn
the art of balancing.* You learn the art of being still while in motion,
of balancing while living in an off-balance world. Genuine spirituality

means living fully into this very moment as the best way to prepare for future moments, while relinquishing the moment that is past.

Both/And Prayer: Living into the Mystery

Spirituality is not about gaining mastery but living into the Mystery. To live into mystery means appreciating the grace in the yin of diminishments as well as the grit in the yang of accomplishments. "Life must be lived forward but it can only be understood backwards," says Danish philosopher Søren Kierkegaard. Do you ever look back at something where you succeeded and ask, *How did I ever do that?* But equally, do you look back at something where you failed and ask, *What was I thinking when I did that?*

YOU ARE STARDUST

According to Rabbi Simcha Bunim of Poland, everyone needs two pockets, with a note in each one. The note in one pocket says, "You are but dust and ashes." In the other, the note says, "For you the universe was created!" To grovel in self-pity or gloat in self-importance is to endanger life's vital balancing. Scientifically and spiritually, we really are stardust and living this paradox is about being what you are.

E-mail bloopers happen to the best and worst. I once forwarded a colleague's confidential e-mail by mistake; it got copied and mailed, unawares, as packing stuffer to our mutual eccentric friend with a copy of one of my books she had ordered. The woman read embarrassing stuff about herself. I felt like total dust; my starry-eyed self crashed. Actually, all of us survived the experience, friendships intact. I'm sharing the incident here because it's "holy humus," and such experiences return me to my dustiness.

For me, when I get too starry, I need to work in my dusty woodshop, see a weird movie, read a crazy fiction story (like Alice Walker's or Flannery O'Connor's) that takes me to the edge of the world. When I get too dusty, I need to play the piano or my Native flute, walk around a lake, or confide in a soul friend. Fill in the blanks for yourself: When I get too starry, I need to…. When I get too dusty, I need to….

Without dust there would be no star. I heard a science lecturer conclude that we humans have dust from ancient rocks swirling around in our DNA: you are hydrogen and clay, she says. That's the mystery of stardust, and prayer means actualizing what you are.

The Lakota Sioux still use a primal prayer that existed long before modern science's "discovery" that we're stardust, an example of primodern—both primal and modern—spirituality. *Mitakuye oyasin!* means, "To all my relations!" The prayer is like a toast to the ancestors and all living things—rocks and rivers, trees and stars, creatures and people.

> To live into mystery means appreciating the grace in the yin of diminishments as well as the grit in the yang of accomplishments.

In the Christian stream, we see a parallel in St. Francis of Assisi's canticle, based on the Hebrew Psalm 148. To sing "All Creatures of Our God and King" is to invite brother sun and sister moon, flowing stream and burning fire, to join with all creatures in praising the divine sovereign One of the universe, "Alleluia!" We are stardust.

FELIX CULPA: A "GOOD MISTAKE"

To claim your stardust, it can help to reflect on a major failed project, or a dumb little thing you did last week, in light of St. Augustine's concept of *felix culpa.* Often it's translated as "happy" or "fortunate" fault, referring to the fall of Adam and Eve. I understand it existentially, as an occasion to realize a backwards gift, as each of us falls from the ideal garden into our own less-than-perfect lives.

I like to translate it as "a good mistake." Only retroactively do you see good coming out of a failed experiment. But even to frame failure as an "experiment" begins to redeem it. Thomas Edison could say he didn't fail, but found two thousand ways how *not* to make the incandescent light bulb. Only in retrospect would Joseph's siblings see how in their evil experiment of selling their dreaming brother into slavery that "God intended it for good, in order to preserve a numerous people" (Genesis 50:20).

Proactively, what we can do is pray to notice flecks of grace in the gaffe or the goof—for it to morph into *felix culpa*, a fortunate failure.

Here's a story of a little good mistake. When my daughter was seventeen, she applied for a summer service trip to Malawi. As her pastor, I signed her application, only to read in the rejection letter that applicants had to be eighteen. But a couple of weeks before the trip, the agency called to say there weren't enough adults, so she and another youth were accepted. The fruit of the mistake was transformational for our daughter's life and vocation, and our family still maintains nurturing friendships with families in Malawi and other African countries.

Someone else's major mistake can be a catalyst for good in your life. In his senior year at Stanford University, all-American tight end Cory Booker was struggling to maintain a Division I football career and high enough grades for graduate school. At the same time, Booker ran a crisis counseling hotline in East Palo Alto, California. When a client threatened to jump off a building, Booker intervened. He had what he calls an epiphany.

"I remember having this profound conversation on the side of the ledge about why he shouldn't jump, and it was almost like a gift to *me*," Booker recalls. "I'll never forget the power I felt when he touched hands for me to pull him over. And at that moment, I realized, 'What am I doing? I don't want to be a football player. I want to get back to the business of making connections with people through my work.'"[1]

As mayor of Newark, New Jersey, Booker's real life-and-death epiphany continues to direct his life. An Oxford Rhodes Scholar with a JD from Yale School of Law, Booker has turned down opportunities most African American men—and any men—can only dream of: offers from top law firms, investment banks, and national appointments. Events always return him to the call that came that day: compassionate public service. "I don't think there's anything more noble about my choice," Booker says. "We do what we love. And I love being in the thick of it."

He's daily in the thick of leading a racially and economically challenging city—making connections with the brokers of power and the broken poor—sometimes under a cloud of assassination rumors. In April 2012, Booker was in the news for rescuing his neighbor's daughter from her burning house.

Living the Paradoxes: Stillness While in Motion

Between the extremes of a purely active or contemplative life lies a paradoxical third way, the Tao of contemplation in action, of stillness in motion. Thomas Merton concludes in his classic *The Seven Storey Mountain*, "Saint Thomas [Aquinas] taught that there were three vocations: that to the active life, that to the contemplative, and a third to the mixture of both, and that this last is superior to the other two."

Hindu Upanishads speak of the third way as a dark night, contrasting people who see the outward world alone as real with those who see the inward world alone as real. "The first leads to a life of action, the second to a life of meditation. But those who combine action and meditation cross the sea of death" (Isha Upanishad 9–11).

The empty space of an extended dark night of the soul may actually act as a reservoir of ministry and space for the fruit of action.

THE TAO OF ABSENCE AND PRESENCE

I offer two examples of contemplation in action in the lives of the eighteenth-century Quaker John Woolman and Mother Teresa of Calcutta.

John Woolman walked on foot up and down the East Coast urging Quakers to free their slaves in the 1700s. He tells in his *Journals* how, through prayer, sometimes when visiting a Friends' Meeting,

"I found no engagement to speak concerning [slaves] and therefore kept silence, finding by experience … to keep pace with the gentle motions of Truth."[2] So effective was Woolman's quiet witness that by the end of the eighteenth century—more than sixty years before the Civil War—Quakers had emancipated their once numerous slaves, a tribute largely to Woolman's influence.

Woolman practiced the paradox of silence and speech, absence and presence. In 1758, after speaking against slavery in the London Grove Meeting, in Pennsylvania, he was invited for dinner at the home of Thomas Woodward. On entering, Woolman observed African servants and learned they were slaves. With neither words nor ill will, he quietly left. When guests gathered at the dinner table, everyone understood the gesture of Woolman's absence. The next morning, Woodward freed all of his slaves. Two years later, the Meeting recorded an official minute that the discontinuance of slavery in the area "hath been visibly blessed with Success."[3]

Courageous Pauper

> Paucity of words,
> audacity in deed.

With the release of her personal writings in *Mother Teresa: Come Be My Light*, the "saint of the streets" made headlines again. The world's popular icon of integrity and love revealed that for over fifty years she felt a sense of absence of the inner peace that she brought to others. Many feel puzzled. What clues can we take from Mother Teresa's soul struggles? How could she give such beautiful pieces of light out of her excruciating night of the soul?

Her amazing life of love seems like even more of a miracle. Two ordinary "miracles" empowered this tiny Albanian nun to move mountains when most human beings would have given up.

First, the process of writing into her doubts served as a life raft to keep her from drowning in the emptiness. Second, behind-the-scenes spiritual guides provided perspective for her to inhabit the emptiness as a valid form of the Presence. She came to understand that her spiritual thirst was her way of identifying with Jesus's darkness when he cried, "My God, my God, why have you forsaken me?" So she embraced Jesus's forsakenness inside herself on behalf of forsaken people. She wrote, "For the first time in 11 years—I have come to love the darkness—for I believe now that it is part of a very, very small part of Jesus's darkness & pain."[4]

Mother Teresa wrote into her darkness as her way of praying and felt Jesus's presence in the least of these. As Indian poet Rabindranath Tagore wrote, "Faith is the bird that feels the light and sings when the dawn is still dark."

THE TAO OF ABILITIES IN DISABILITIES

The ability to find gifts in disabilities is one of the mystery miracles of this Spirit life. By sharing my learning differences, bipolar struggles, vocational upheavals, and parenting hassles, others seem to find their own experiences validated. Many tell me they have never heard such vulnerable places named from lectern or pulpit, and never as an invitation to mine bits of grace in the grit.

Harold Wilke was born with no arms. In his youth he felt called to be a minister, but church officials said, how could he hold children to baptize them? Or hold the bread and cup to celebrate Communion? So he enlisted elders to hold the babies, to hold the loaf and chalice. He used his very disability to multiply the gifts in the community and around the world.

> The ability to find gifts in disabilities is one of the mystery miracles of this Spirit life.

Wilke pioneered in disabilities awareness as he spoke at church, civic, and worldwide conferences. Thus he paved the way for the 1990 signing of the Americans with Disabilities Act at the White House, where he gave the blessing. Next time you cross a street at a city stoplight and notice the recessed sidewalk for wheelchairs or see an elevator at street level, you can thank this man born without arms.

THE TAO OF FRIENDSHIP

The Sufi Muslim poet Rumi describes genuine friendship with the paradoxical phrase in his poem title: "Fierce Courtesy." When Rumi speaks of the connection to the "Friend," we might understand it as the image of the divine Friend, as well as his soul friend Shams, who had thrown Rumi's books in a river.

Sometimes a human friend crosses your path, and you wake up to find your life turned around 180 degrees. In *Tolkien and C.S. Lewis: The Gift of Friendship*, Colin Duriez writes of Lewis, "Friendship with Tolkien, he found, shook him fully awake, out of the cold dream of materialism." Lewis himself used a phrase similar to Rumi's to describe his wife Joy Davidman's brief life and death, calling the time "a severe mercy."

Rumi's "Fierce Courtesy" provides a metaphor to see even frightening experiences or dreams as spiritual friends. Just as you pull a child's hand back from a hot stove or from crossing a treacherous street, a fierce episode may shake you loose to see a new vision. In "The Guest House," Rumi bids us to welcome any experience as "a guide from beyond."

THE TAO OF PARENTING AND LEADERSHIP

One summer we returned to our home to find a cardinal had built her nest in a lilac bush outside our dining room window. She laid three eggs. Ten days after they hatched, on Saturday morning, I sensed the fledglings would leave. I noticed the mother flitting to the nest only briefly, then absenting herself to settle on a spruce tree some fifty feet away—there to watch with nary a move.

Midmorning, one little bird struggled up onto the edge of the nest, where it rested for some time, then spread its wings, promptly plummeting to a branch below. There it sat for some time, gathering its strength, then spread its wings, and with great energy and acuity ascended to a branch a bit higher than the nest. Once again, it rested, summoning its strength. *There's got to be a third movement to this symphony,* I said to myself. And sure enough, it soon spread its wings and soared away. With virtually the same three movements—down, up, and away—each little fledgling made its debut. In late afternoon, the mother cardinal left the spruce tree. I may have spied her once later.

The cardinal's story beautifully illustrates nature's way of developing resilience in young creatures: mother nurturing directly, but then hiding out, attentively observing, loving her little ones from a distance.

On one level, the story is a parable of God—what Martin Luther called the "hidden" God—loving us, without our awareness, into becoming our own best selves. Is it not a parable of the soul's dark night, when it may seem we no longer experience the felt intimacy of the Presence? Then God loves us at a distance and yet at the same time takes up residence within us. For so short a time the mother had imparted "cardinal virtue"—in the old sense, meaning "power"—to her young ones, through birthing them and nurturing them, then leaving them. For me, it represents the Christ story—the one who comes, lives, and loves among us, and leaves in order to send the Spirit to empower us within.

The cardinal's story also represents a model for healthy parenting and leadership: to live, and love, and nurture a resilient spirit in those we care about and work with—and to learn to love by practicing creative absence as well as presence. The ancient Chinese *Tao Te Ching* reminds us, "Do your work, then step back"—as the only path to serenity.

> The ancient Chinese *Tao Te Ching* reminds us, "Do your work, then step back"—as the only path to serenity.

It is the same message in the Jewish Kabbalah, of God stepping back (*tzimtzum*) from creation to make space for the creatures; in Christianity, of Christ emptying the divine self (*kenosis*) to rise in power. Genuine spirituality nurtures a healthy rhythm of emptying and expanding, giving and receiving, absence and presence, contemplation and action, holding and releasing.

In the classic Eastern icon of the Virgin of Vladimir, you notice Mary has one hand holding the seemingly miniature adult Christ child, while the other is extended upward, releasing (while many Western Madonnas portray both hands clutching). It's as if Mary envisions her child already mature, greater than herself—a gift to be held lightly.

For parenting and for leadership, I see in this icon a wonderfully holistic paradox, integrating male and female, child and elder, student and mentor. I look at my children and students and think: *you are my teachers.* Genuine eldering involves a mutual mentoring, as my generation needs to spend time with younger generations, and learn from each other. Kything prayer is a way to practice this art of holding and releasing (see Prayer Practice 9).

THE TAO OF SIMPLICITY AND COMPLEXITY

Here in Crestone, Colorado, where I've come away to pray and write, I hold a circular stone that fits in the palm of my hand. I think of William Blake's line "to see the world in a grain of sand." The stone is so small, yet it's a hologram of the universe, so simple for me to hold, yet so complex that it holds billions of years of geological history. In my hand, it's a talking stone, meant to hear many stories. In the hand of my geologist friend Jake, it's meant to be analyzed. The North is the time for the second naiveté, to celebrate the wedding of our primal knowing and our modern knowledge—simple stories I will invite and complex scientific data Jake will dig up.

Maybe primodernity is the same thing as simplexity, a term made popular by Jeffrey Kluger in *Simplexity: Why Simple Things Become Complex (and How Complex Things Can Be Made Simple).* Concepts like *via negativa* and *via positiva* may sound complex, but it's as simple as saying that we meet God in dark times and light times. In R.E.M.'s "Losing My Religion," Michael Stipe sings about "standing in the corner" and "standing in the spotlight." Simplexity means both can happen at once: the shaming incident may contain the spark that lights your passion.

Frederick Douglass, a child slave who would become a brilliant writer, educator, and orator, overheard his master say it was a dangerous thing for a slave to learn to read and write. "From that moment, I understood the pathway from slavery to freedom," wrote Douglass. A mysterious inkling, meant to cause shame, acted as the goad to achieve his treasure.

On my last day teaching a class on prayer, a quiet man came to me and said, "You gave me lots of new ideas. But I'm a Twelve Step guy, and for me praying is pretty simple: *Help me*, *I'm sorry*, *Forgive me*, and *Thank you*." I've pondered how the same two-word prayers, when spoken to another human being, might simultaneously be prayers to God. And I've pondered how such simple praying seems so complex that many find it impossible. Why?

"If in your lifetime the only prayer you offer is 'thank you,' that would suffice," says Meister Eckhart. Why do I still struggle to say "thank you" to another human being? I think it's because to do so puts me in a position of humility, makes me dependent on someone outside myself. I've pondered, too, how my student's simple Twelve Step prayers are really complex. They're similar to ancient *ho'o pono pono*, meaning "to make right twice"—forgiving and loving yourself *and* another. These simple Hawaiian Polynesian spiritual practices prove highly effective in restoring family systems and reconciling cultural differences. We can practice family rituals of thanks that unite the paradoxes of receiving and giving, breaking and blessing (see Prayer Practice 20).

THE TAO OF HIGH-TECH AND HIGH-TOUCH

Cool computer screens and impersonal institutions leave tech generations starving for spiritual intimacy in authentic community. "The primal scream of postmodern spirituality is for primal experiences of God," says Leonard Sweet in *Quantum Spirituality*. As some of us offer spiritual companioning via the Internet (using smartphones or Skype), we're rediscovering the ancient spiritual "web" of Native tradition virtually alive. Three decades ago, I never dreamed that my life mission to be a "link" between the Word and the world would tap into a virtual "link" that connects me, at the click of my keypad, with ancient wisdom and contemporary world issues like TED (Technology, Entertainment, Design), on behalf of God's world. My website—www.LinkYourSpirituality.com—helps me live out that mission. Primodern spirituality is a call to young generations to integrate yet unimagined forms of future high-tech learnings and primal high-touch yearnings.

THE TAO OF QUESTIONS AND STORIES

A good question at the right time can change the course of your life, and a good story at the right time can change someone else's life—or vice versa. Discerning when to ask and when to tell is essential to the art of loving your neighbor. Quaker wisdom, once again, is helpful. When it first occurs to you to speak, you ask, is this thought just for *me*? You hold it back, and if it comes a second time, you ask, is it for me *and* for those present? If it knocks yet a third time on the door of your consciousness, you ask, is it for me *and* for those present, and is it for *now*?

By practicing this wisdom, I've known moments when a story I thought was foolish connects on a subliminal level with the person I'm with—to open up their own insight—and moments when questioning myself led to a life-giving insight. Questions and stories embody the yin and the yang for practicing the paradoxes in prayerful living (see Prayer Practice 21).

Cultivating Paradoxical Prayer

Incorporating paradoxes in your prayers can script the psyche and predispose the mind to look for surprise moments of common ground even in hostile political and theological conversations. I offer these couplets as grist for the prayer practices in this book.

COMPLAINING AND THANKING

Psalms provide a template for honest to God prayer, using multiple intelligences to express all the moods of the soul. In "Bittersweet," seventeenth-century English poet George Herbert prays boldly:

> Ah, my dear angry Lord....
> I shall bewail, approve,
> I shall complain yet praise,
> And all my sour-sweet days
> I shall lament and love.

Crying, shouting, and laughing may not sound contemplative, yet can often lead to cathartic cleansing, preparing the soul for sacred silence.

WORDS AND WORDLESS

I'm advocating multiple forms of wordless prayer, especially silence and gestures. John Woolman's social gesture of leaving his seat empty embodied a silent message to free his host's household slaves. Using physical gestures to create a "chalice prayer" nonverbally gathers up paradoxes of life (see Prayer Practice 22).

Written prayers create a vital way to voice desires of the heart and thoughts of the mind, and to listen to spaces between the words. Wherever I write, in a desert hermitage, or in a monastery, or in my Denver home, a prayer poem I composed in the 1990s at the Jesuit Spiritual Center in Wernersville, Pennsylvania, expresses paradoxes of my writing life: contemplation and action, burden and gift, the hermitage within myself and any place where I write. Merton played with paradoxes, speaking of himself, like

Jonah in the whale, as living in the belly of a paradox. I invite you to script paradoxes in your prayers.

Writer's Asceticism

> Merton-like I hide away
> to pray to write and pray
> in this my hermitage,
> to birth my heritage:
> the gift of the burden,
> the burden of the gift.

SELF AND OTHERS

Intercession is the religious term for prayers for others, and sometimes the spiritual energy you spend on behalf of another pays a backward dividend of enriching your own soul. A middle-aged spiritual companion arrived with a vampire book and said, "I'm reading this because my teenage son is reading it. I thought it might be a way for me to get inside his head and understand him a bit more." The idea spawned my own imagination. The next time I got in my car and heard a hard-rock radio station my son had programmed, I thought, *I'm praying for my son!* Listening to a radio station, reading a book, seeing a movie, or doing everyday chores with special intention for another can be creative ways to hold a person in your heart (see Prayer Practice 23).

BODY AND SPIRIT

Your body, including your brain and breath, is a "temple of the Holy Spirit," according to the apostle Paul (1 Corinthians 6:19). Likewise Basava, a twelfth-century Hindu reformer, reflects on the body as a sacred temple.

> The rich will make temples for Siva:
> What shall I, a poor man, do?
> My legs are pillars, the body is a shrine,
> The head is the cupola, of gold.[5]

If we really listen to our temple-bodies, can we hear echoes of lost liturgies of our lives? (See Prayer Practice 24).

What Makes Secular Stuff Prayer?

What determines if everyday human expressions of your yearnings are really prayer? Nineteenth-century English Jesuit poet Gerard Manley Hopkins gives a simple answer: "All things give God glory if you mean they should."

I've often told the story of a squeamish chaplain visiting a woman with end-stage cancer. He thought he was going to throw up, so he sat for several minutes with his head in his hands, then felt so embarrassed he left. The next day the woman reported it was the most meaningful visit she ever had; she didn't want to talk, and that chaplain just sat and prayed for her in silence. On hearing this story, someone said, "But the chaplain wasn't really praying, was he?" Such gut-wrenching identity with another's pain *is* your praying, yearning with biblical "bowels of mercies" (*splagchna* in Greek); it's visceral prayer.

> Gut-wrenching identity with another's pain *is* your praying, yearning with biblical "bowels of mercies" (*splagchna* in Greek); it's visceral prayer.

So what makes secular experiences spiritual? In her *Journal of a Solitude*, May Sarton offers this perspective:

> If one looks long enough at almost anything, looks with absolute attention at a flower, a stone, the bark of a tree, grass, snow, a cloud, something like revelation takes place. Something is "given," and perhaps that something is always a reality outside the self. We are aware of God only when we cease to be aware of ourselves, not in the negative sense of denying the self, but in the sense of losing self in admiration and joy.[6]

Think of prayer as a laboratory to notice sacred particulars in secular stuff, even after the fact. I hope you reframe what you thought were only mundane or even profane experiences, to see pinholes of a spiritual eclipse—"This may be part of my spiritual journey"—though it would have been too bright to see directly at the time.

Seven Practices for Integrating Both/And Spiritual Living

The goal of honest to God prayer is to restore the soul and integrate healthy spirituality in areas of life that too easily get compartmentalized. I offer seven guidelines for practices to fulfill this over time:

1. Engage in holistic prayer practices that express exhilaration and exhaustion and nurture your own soul;
2. Pray with sacred texts and spiritual readings to connect with the contexts of your active life, work, and relationships;
3. Balance your schedule with sabbath and service, silence and speech, solitude and community;
4. Commit to spiritual companioning (one-on-one or group) and nurturing healthy friendships with appropriate boundaries;
5. Transform failure through prayer by mining gifts in weaknesses and strengths;
6. Integrate the mystical, political, intellectual, and physical arenas of your life; and
7. Develop and follow your life mission to link your passion with the world's need.

The Tree of Life: A Parable

I return to the primal paradox of contemplation and action: the tree of life. Most of you reading this are discerning your *being* in the Sacred in the grit of your *doing* in the world—dancing with paradoxes of spirituality and sexuality, feasting and fasting, sabbath and service, complexity and simplicity. So I offer this for you as my prayer parable.

> *Master*: As a tree dies cut off from its roots, so you will die in the midst of worldly business. To live you need to return to your roots.
>
> *Disciple*: Should I leave my business and go into a monastery?
>
> *Master*: By no means! The roots need the branches to give life. Stay in the world and return to your heart.

If you return to the deepest yearning of your heart, you will not be able for long to avoid the yearning of the world for long—and of the One who is the resilient Mystery at the heart of existence—honest to God.

Wherever inklings of transforming Mystery happen—in a fleeting moment of worship, in a painful glimpse of self in public, in the ecstasy of a child's insight, in a self-forgetting act of altruism—you've tasted joy in sacrifice; you've experienced what for me is Eucharist: crumbs of life's broken bread have dropped in on your world to bless you and the cosmos. Moments of honest to God prayer are at once moments when the soul is renewed while you're extending hospitality—even if it is to the stranger within yourself.

Practices for Cultivating Paradox

Sounds of Technology, Nature—and Silence

Find a really noisy place outside, like a bench near a mall parking lot, a street corner, or an expressway. Sit ... observe colors, light, movements ... close your eyes and slow down your breathing.... Notice the sounds of technology (vehicles, planes, radios).... Then see if you can hear even faint sounds of nature (birds, insects, wind).... Place your index fingers in each ear for a few minutes ... then remove them. Finally, listen beyond the noises to the sound of silence. If you can't, simply invite the distractions in as part of your prayers. Conclude by opening your eyes and reflecting on this experience.

Option: Turn up music loudly to practice the same exercise inside or outside, by yourself or with a group (but give consideration for your neighbors!).

Prayer Practice 20

Table Blessing with Head, Heart, and Hands

This is my daily bread (*hold out cupped hands, palms up*);

Take it (*lift hands slightly, palms still up*);

Bless it (*place one cupped hand over the other*);

Break it (*twist hands as if breaking a loaf*);

Give it to everyone I meet today (*extend hands outward*).

Leader: Invite the group to repeat words and gestures; then repeat gestures without words.

Prayer Practice 21

Practicing Questions, Telling Stories

Seize occasions to experiment in the coming week. Try making an observation and/or asking a question instead of giving an insight: "I noticed a phrase you used (repeating what the person said); I wonder, what's that about?" Or, if a story comes to mind more than once while conversing, share it. Gently ask if there might be any connection for the other person. Allow pauses to draw you deeper into trusting love in the Ground of your being.

Prayer Practice 22

Chalice Prayer

Hold your hands open: meditate on gifts they offer.
Fold your hands as in a gesture of prayer.
Gently lift them out of the line of sight,
then open them to form a chalice,
the cup of your life.
Drink deeply of
your cup:
breathe
in and out.
Bring the hands down
to form an X over your heart,
Love entering anew to bless you:
breathe in... out... release and open hands,
so that your life may be a blessing to the world.

Repeat each gesture with one word or phrase: *offering* (hands folded); *opening* (hands forming chalice); *being blessed* (hands crossed on heart); *blessing* (hands releasing).

Prayer Practice 23

A Radio Station, Book, Movie, or Mundane Tasks as Prayer

Here's a way to walk in the moccasins of a loved one or friend you want to understand better: *Listen to someone's favorite radio station, read the person's favorite book, or see a movie the person would like* (by yourself, or together). Maybe you will converse about it, maybe not. But if it helps you walk with your friend and understand the person, then it is prayer. (In Christian tradition it would be called an *intercessory* prayer, that is, your soul's concern offered on behalf of another.)

Option: Engage in a mundane task as prayer. As you mow grass, take out garbage, clean a toilet, or make a bed, engage in the task with mindfulness. Dedicate such times "with special intention" for fellow laborers, migrant workers, restaurant servers, housekeeping staff—for any who earn a living doing manual labor.

Idea: Using your journal, reflect on a past work experience or service project, being attentive to any edge of spiritual growth. Everything becomes a prayer if you mean it so.

Prayer Practice 24

Cultivating Paradox: Do Things the Opposite Way

Take a different route to work or school. Put on the opposite sock first. Zip your jacket with your left hand (or right hand if you are left-handed). Eat a meal with the opposite hand. Brush your teeth after having sex (or before, whichever breaks a pattern). Try some of these for about a week, then reflect on the experiences. Notice if simple physical exercises open up a new awareness of the mystery of paradoxical spiritual insights.[7]

Bring It All Together

Morning Prayer in Four Directions

"Faithfulness will spring up from the ground,
and righteousness will look down from the sky."
—PSALM 85:11

"People will come from east and west, from north and
south, and will eat in the kingdom of God."
—LUKE 13:29

"The start of life's journey, the new day, is in the
East.... It is the place of beginnings, first light—and the
possibility of starting again."
—JOSEPH BRUCHAC, *NATIVE WISDOM*

The themes of this book are echoed in nearly every primal spiritual
tradition: the morning, noon, afternoon, and night of life. The
grounding and process for these—awareness, empowerment, relinquishment, and paradox—come together holistically when you place
your feet on the ground and integrate these into your own interior
being. (If you are physically unable to stand for this exercise, then you
may simulate the gestures from a sitting position.)

This four directions exercise adapts Native American traditions with tai chi and optional Christian expressions, as you face the four points of the compass (also corresponding to the four seasons; see "Prologue"). The East represents the *childhood of life*—and as such may be a prayer for the healing of childhood memories, or for children of the world; the South, the *noon of life*, burgeoning youthful and mid-life vocational and sexual energies, and for youth and young adults; the West, the *afternoon of life*, times of diminishments and of letting go, and creation and for elders; the North, *dying—direction and discernment*—or the "dark night of the soul": also prayer for persons going through such times. Each can be dedicated to persons or nations in that direction. (You may engage in this practice at sunrise or in early morning by facing the East to mark new beginnings; or adapt the prayer at noon by facing the South to pray for vision and vocation, and so on—ending in the direction that completes the four compass points.)

Face the East

Looking straight ahead, roll your eyes to the right, stretching your peripheral vision; then the same to the left; upward; downward; all the while keeping your head still, looking straight forward as if seeing in all directions at once!

Option: You may then sing or recite a morning hymn, poem, or prayer, such as "Morning has Broken."

A. Facing the *East*, say to yourself, *"Left wing as a bird in flight."*

Bend knees slightly (not stiff) and gently lift left foot, standing on your right foot with knees slightly bent, and left arm akimbo—placing left hand with forefingers facing front, thumb facing back, curved around the top of your left hip.

Say, *"Right wing as in flight."*

Gently lift right foot, standing on your left foot with knees slightly bent, and right arm akimbo—right hand curved around the top of right hip, with forefingers facing front and thumb facing back.

Say, *"Both wings as in flight."*

Stand on both feet with knees slightly bent, both arms akimbo, and each hand curved around the top of each hip (as above).

Fold hands in front of you in traditional prayer posture, gently lifting folded hands pointed skyward, above your head.

Exhaling, slowly make a graceful bow toward the earth, hands still folded; then open palms toward the earth, kneel or squat, while saying, *"And father sky comes down to greet mother earth and bless the earth with gifts of sun and rain, heat and light, air and moisture."*

Place open palms down on the earth (or floor), perhaps even kissing the earth affectionately (or an "air kiss," lips not touching earth), all breath now exhaled, hold.

Turn palms upward, as if to make a scoop for earth or water, begin to inhale, saying, *"And draw from the earth ..."*

Standing, bring the scooped hands up to your chest below the heart (hold breath); then exhale, thrusting fingertips straight forward, saying, *"... and give back to the world."*

Take a step slightly right and front, then with feet together, and hands still extended, scribe a big circle with your hands *from bottom to top* ( ) to simulate the sun (as if drawing simultaneously the two halves of the circle, one with each hand, on an imaginary blackboard!)

With hands at the "top" of your circle, inhale, and say, *"Draw from the sky ..."*

Pull hands down and in, fingers touching each other, palms placed on your chest, hold; Exhale, saying, *"... and give back to the world ..."*—thrusting fingertips straight out.

Inhale while bringing hands back to chest and say *"... and draw from the circle of your life, your self to your true self ..."*

Form an X shape as if to "hug yourself"—left hand embracing right shoulder, right hand on left shoulder, feeling God's blessing on your whole being, hold and say, *"... and be renewed."* You might also hold a loved one in your heart with hands in this position, picturing their face.

With an exhaled breath, release hands forward in cupped position, lifting other causes and countries. Release hands to sides.

Face the South

B. Position the right foot at a right angle, and take one large step to your right, turning to face the *South*, and bring the left foot parallel, both facing South—then repeat motions as above in A: *"Left wing as in flight—Right wing as in flight—Both wings as in flight. And the sky comes down to greet the earth and bless the earth with gifts of light and moisture—Draw from the earth—and give back to the world—Draw from the sky—and give back to the world—and be renewed."*

You might also hold a loved one in your heart with hands in this position, picturing their face.

With an exhaled breath, release hands forward in cupped position, lifting other causes and countries. Release hands to sides.

Face the West

C. Position the right foot at a right angle, and take one step to your right, turning to face the *West*, and bring the left foot parallel, both facing West—then repeat motions, as above.

In the afternoon of life, the shadow comes to the fore: so it is a time for embracing the shadow parts of oneself. (Also, facing the West I often think of national environmental treasures such as the Grand Canyon, Yosemite, or Yellowstone, in the western US. I often pray for the healing of the environment, wildlife, and eco-systems—so much a part of all Native traditions.)

Finish as in A and B.

Face the North

D. Position the right foot at a right angle, and take one step to your right, turning to face the *North*, and bring the left foot parallel, both facing North—then repeat motions, as above. (Often I pray for various nation-states in the four directions, or for someone who lives to the South, or West, etc., or for myself in the summer of my life, or for someone in the evening of her or his life, or—thinking of the North star, *for guidance* for myself or another person; or for appreciating *the depth of life* (only at night can we see the depth, mystery, and beauty of the universe); or for *someone facing death*—or whatever associations come to mind. As to exact positions and movements, some I have borrowed, some are my own.)

Finish as in A and B.

E. At the very end, still facing the North with hands released from embracing yourself, take one big step back and you will have moved to the center of your "circle"—representing the whole cosmos. You will have made *the primal pattern of a cross with your feet*—a prayer for the good news of peace to go forth into all the world.

Option: At this point you may make the sign of the cross, traditionally with the right hand, saying the words:

"In the name of the Father ..."—touching the forehead, dedicating the mind and intellect;

"... and of the Son"—touching lower stomach, dedicating the passion and compassion;

"... and of the Holy Spirit"—bringing the hand up through the heart, then from one shoulder to the other crossing at the throat, dedicating the breath and voice;

"... one God, Mother of us all!"—bringing hand back to the center of your chest, holding it a moment.

Note: These words preserve the traditional Trinitarian baptismal formula (Matthew 28:19), yet they add: *"... one God"*—(the *Shema*, Deuteronomy 6:4), the true meaning of Trinity (tri-unity), also the scriptural phrase used by Julian of Norwich—*"mother of us all."*

Acknowledgments

Gratitude is such an amazing quality that manifests itself in compassion and a bountiful harvest of friendships. Writing is a form of praying, and I never really write alone, because I've discovered in the process that we are all one.

Honest to God Prayer has been gestating since the late 1980s (though I wrote several books between then and now), and I want to acknowledge some of its many midwives. I think of Myron Ebersole, my chaplain supervisor in 1987 at Penn State's Hershey Medical Center, who invited me for to a weeklong retreat at Shalem Institute in Washington, DC, resulting in my training there. At Shalem, Gerald May, MD, Tilden Edwards, and Rose Mary Dougherty, SSND, became mentors, along with countless others who have crossed my path. I am grateful to Edwin Sanders, SJ, Carl Dincher, SJ, Sister Marian Dolores Frantz, IHM, my midlife spiritual guides, and to colleagues Rabbi Rami Shapiro, Rabbi Carl Choper, Belva Brown Jordan, Augustino Tierramar, and Luther Smith, who expanded for me an appreciation of broader interfaith and cross-cultural connections, while at the same time inviting me to deepen my own ancestral and Christian heritage.

I thank my editor, Emily Wichland, vice president of Editorial and Production at SkyLight Paths, whose keen feedback sometimes upended chunks of dense text, which I then reworked to bear fruits of more light and love.

I recall an early pivotal moment when my colleague William Rader listened as I spun out the four themes of this book: he told me I *must* publish this. With my wife, Fredrika, and countless spiritual companions, I've experienced the synergy of mutual insights, encouraging my writing journey—and your journey into prayer.

Notes

Integrating Native American and Ignatian Spiritual Streams

1. See Joseph Bruchac, ed., *Native Wisdom* (San Francisco: HarperSanFrancisco, 1995).

2. For a summary of Ignatius's *Spiritual Exercises*, see Kent Ira Groff, *Facing East, Praying West: Poetic Reflections on the Spiritual Exercises* (New York: Paulist Press, 2010).

Chapter One. Waking Up to Reality: The Grounding for Awareness

1. Steve Jobs, "2005 Stanford Commencement Address," *Forbes*, www.forbes.com/sites/davidewalt/2011/10/05/steve-jobs-2005-stanford-commencement-address.

2. For several informative articles on the tree of life theme, see *Parabola* (Fall 1989), "The Tree of Life."

3. Simplexity is a term made popular by Jeffrey Kluger in *Simplexity: Why Simple Things Become Complex (and How Complex Things Can Be Made Simple)* (New York: Hyperion, 2008).

4. Rumi, *The Glance: Rumi's Songs of Soul-Meeting*, tr. Coleman Barks (New York: Viking, 1999), 83.

Chapter Two. Living Awake to What Is: The Process of Awareness

1. Hafiz, *The Gift: Poems by Hafiz the Great Sufi Master*, tr. Daniel Ladinsky (New York: Penguin Compass, 1999), 107.

2. Howard Gardner, *Multiple Intelligences: New Horizons* (New York: Basic Books, 2006); and *The Unschooled Mind: How Children Think & How Schools Should Teach* (New York: Basic Books, 1991). See also *Creating Minds: An Anatomy of Creativity Seen Through the Lives of Freud, Einstein, Picasso, Stravinsky, Eliot, Graham, and Gandhi* (New York: Basic Books, 1993); and "Howard Gardner's Multiple Intelligences Theory," www.pbs.org/wnet/gperf/education/ed_mi_overview.html.

3. Adapted from "A Mitzvah Gives Life" in Eugene Labovitz and Annette Labovitz, *Time for My Soul: A Treasury of Stories for Our Holy Days* (Northvale, NJ: J. Aronson, 1987), 240.

4. Kathleen Norris, *Dakota: A Spiritual Geography* (New York: Houghton Mifflin, 1993), 22.

Chapter Three. Claiming Possibilities: The Grounding for Empowerment

1. C. S. Lewis, *Letters to Malcolm: Chiefly on Prayer* (New York: Harcourt, 1992), 21–22.

2. Philip Schultz, "Words Failed, Then Saved Me," *New York Times*, September 3, 2011.

3. Stephen Chapin Garner and Jerry Thornell, *Scattering Seeds: Cultivating Church Vitality* (Herndon, VA: The Alban Institute, 2012).

4. Rachel Naomi Remen, *Kitchen Table Wisdom: Stories That Heal* (New York: Riverhead Books, 1996), 248–251.

Chapter Four. Embracing Dreams: The Process of Empowerment

1. Helen Knox Murphy, *Common Nobility: A Family Story* (Houston: Kitchen Table Top Publishers, 2002), 23.

2. *Alcoholics Anonymous: The Story of How Thousands of Men and Women Have Recovered*, the so-called "AA Big Book" (New York: AA World Services, Inc., 2001), 87–88.

Chapter Five. Negative Capability: The Grounding for Relinquishment

1. This story is adapted from Thich Nhat Hanh, *Being Peace* (Berkeley, CA: Parallax Press, 1987), 42–43.

2. Ernest Kurtz and Katherine Ketcham, *The Spirituality of Imperfection* (New York: Bantam Books, 1992), 1.

3. For more on a Christian interpretation of *kenosis*, see Jurgen Moltmann, *God in Creation: An Ecological Doctrine of Creation* (London: SCM Press, 1985), 86.

4. John Keats, *The Letters of John Keats, Vol. I*, ed. Maurice Buxton Forman (Oxford: Oxford University Press, 1931), 77.

Chapter Six. Shedding Attachments: The Process of Relinquishment

1. Joyce Rupp, *Praying Our Goodbyes* (Notre Dame, IN: Ave Maria Press, 1988), 83–93.

2. See Jan Hoffman, *Clearness Committees and Their Use in Spiritual Discernment* (Philadelphia: Quaker Press of FGC, 1996); Patricia Loring, *Spiritual Discernment: The Context and Goal of Clearness Committees* (Wallingford, PA: Pendle Hill Pamphlet, 1992); and Parker J. Palmer, *Let Your Life Speak: Listening for the Voice of Vocation* (San Francisco: Jossey-Bass, 2000).

3. See Eugene Gendlin, *Focusing* (New York: Bantam Books, 1981) and Ann Weiser Cornell, *The Power of Focusing* (Oakland, CA: New Harbinger Publications, 1996).

Chapter Seven. Rediscovering Mystery: The Grounding for Paradox

1. See this summary of Paul Ricoeur's idea of the second naiveté: www.exploring-spiritual-development.com/Paul-Ricoeur.html.

2. William Butler Yeats, from "Vacillation," in *Collected Works by William Butler Yeats (1865–1939)*, http://classiclit.about.com/library/bl-etexts/wbyeats/bl-wbye-vac.htm.

3. *Bhagavad-Gita: The Song of God*, tr. Swami Prabhavananda and Christopher Isherwood (Madras/Chennai, India: Sri Ramakrishna Math, n.d.), 114 (adapted for inclusive language).

4. Elie Wiesel, *The Town Beyond the Wall* (New York: Avon Books, 1964), 123.

5. Karen Armstrong, *A History of God: The 4,000-Year Quest of Judaism, Christianity and Islam* (New York: Ballantine Books, 1993), 187–88.

Chapter Eight. The Active Contemplative Life: The Process of Paradox

1. Susan Headden. 2006. "The Guy in the Thick of It." *U.S. News & World Report*, April 24.

2. John Woolman, *The Journal and Major Essays of John Woolman*, ed. Phillips P. Moulton (Richmond, IN: Friends United Press, 1989), 70.

3. See Elton Trueblood, *The New Man for Our Time* (New York: Harper & Row, 1970), 48.

4. Brian Kolodiejchuk, ed., *Mother Teresa: Come Be My Light* (New York: Doubleday, 2007), 208.

5. *Forty Days to Begin a Spiritual Life: Today's Most Inspiring Teachers Help You on Your Way*, created by the editors of SkyLight Paths (Woodstock, VT: SkyLight Paths Publishing, 2002), 21.

6. May Sarton, *Journal of a Solitude* (New York: W. W. Norton & Company, 1973), 99.

7. For "doing things the opposite way" I am indebted to Dr. Kang Yup Na, professor of religion and New Testament at Westminster College, New Wilmington, Pennsylvania. Na draws from his own Korean background and ancient Asian and biblical traditions.

Resources for
Further Reading

Prayer and the Spiritual Life

Bourgeault, Cynthia. *Centering Prayer and Inner Awakening.* New York: Cowley Publications, 2004.

Epperly, Bruce G. and Katherine Gould Epperly. *Tending to the Holy: The Practice of the Presence of God in Ministry.* Herndon, VA: The Alban Institute, 2009.

Groff, Kent Ira. *Active Spirituality: A Guide for Seekers and Ministers.* Herndon, VA: The Alban Institute, 1993.

————. *What Would I Believe If I Didn't Believe Anything?: A Handbook for Spiritual Orphans.* San Francisco: Jossey-Bass, 2003.

Hays, Edward M. *Prayers for a Planetary Pilgrim: A Personal Manual for Prayer and Ritual.* Notre Dame, IN: Forest of Peace Publishing, 1989.

Johnston, William, ed. *The Cloud of Unknowing.* New York: Doubleday, 2005.

Lawrence of the Resurrection, Brother. *The Practice of the Presence of God.* trans. John J. Delaney. New York: Image Books Doubleday, 1977.

Lewis, C. S. *Letters to Malcolm, Chiefly on Prayer.* Orlando, FL: Harcourt, Inc., 1964.

Paintner, Christine Valters. *Lectio Divina—The Sacred Art: Transforming Words and Images into Heart-Centered Prayer.* Woodstock, VT: SkyLight Paths Publishing, 2011.

Savary, Louis M. and Patricia H. Berne. *Kything: The Art of Spiritual Presence.* New York: Paulist Press, 1988.

Underhill, Evelyn. *The Spiritual Life.* Harrisburg, PA: Morehouse Publishing, 1999.

Wuellner, Flora Slosson. *Prayer and Our Bodies.* Nashville, TN: Upper Room Books, 1987.

Interfaith Sources

Bhagavad-Gita: The Song of God. trans. Swami Prabhavananda and Christopher Isherwood, intro. by Aldous Huxley. New York: New American Library (Penguin Group), 2002.

Borg, Marcus, ed. *Jesus & Buddha: The Parallel Sayings.* Berkeley, CA: Ulysses Press, 2002.

Bruchac, Joseph, ed. *Native Wisdom.* San Francisco: HarperSanFrancisco, 1995.

Celtic Daily Prayer. ed. The Northumbria Community. San Francisco: HarperSanFrancisco, 2002.

The Koran. trans. and with notes by N. J. Dawood. New York: Penguin Books, 2006.

Kushner, Lawrence. *Eyes Remade for Wonder.* Woodstock, VT: Jewish Lights, 1998.

Lao-tzu. *Tao Te Ching.* ed. and trans. Stephen Mitchell. New York: HarperPerennial, 1991.

Nhat Hanh, Thich. *Living Buddha, Living Christ.* New York: Riverhead Books, 1995.

Wilson, Andrew, ed. *World Scripture: A Comparative Anthology of Sacred Texts.* St. Paul, MN: Paragon House, 1995.

Poetry

Eliot, T. S. *Four Quartets.* New York: Harcourt Brace Jovanovich, 1971.

Eliot, T. S. *T. S. Eliot: Selected Poems.* New York: Harcourt Brace Jovanovich, 1964.

Groff, Kent Ira. *Facing East, Praying West: Poetic Reflections on The Spiritual Exercises.* New York: Paulist Press, 2010.

Hafiz. *The Gift: Poems by Hafiz the Great Sufi Master.* trans. Daniel Ladinsky. New York: Penguin Compass, 1999.

Oliver, Mary. *New and Selected Poems.* Boston: The Beacon Press, 1992.

Rumi, Jalal al-Din. *The Glance: Songs of Soul-Meeting.* trans. Coleman Barks with Nevit Ergin. New York: Viking, 1999.

Additional Resources

Bridges, William. *Transitions: Making Sense of Life's Changes*. Cambridge, MA: Da Capo Press, 2004.

Cornell, Ann Weiser. *The Power of Focusing: A Practical Guide to Emotional Self-Healing*. Oakland, CA: New Harbinger Publications, 1996.

De Mello, Anthony. *One Minute Wisdom*. New York: Doubleday, 1985.

Gardner, Howard. *Multiple Intelligences: New Horizons*. New York: Basic Books, 2006.

————. *Creating Minds: An Anatomy of Creativity Seen Through the Lives of Freud, Einstein, Picasso, Stravinsky, Eliot, Graham, and Gandhi*. New York: Basic Books, 1993.

Gendlin, Eugene T. *Focusing*. New York: Bantam Books, 1981.

Kluger, Jeffrey. *Simplexity: Why Simple Things Become Complex (and How Complex Things Can Be Made Simple)*. New York: Hyperion, 2008.

Merton, Thomas. *The Seven Storey Mountain*. New York: Harcourt Brace Jovanovich, 1976.

Palmer, Parker J. "The Clearness Committee: A Communal Approach to Discernment." www.couragerenewal.org/parker/writings/clearness-committee.

Remen, Rachel Naomi. *Kitchen Table Wisdom: Stories That Heal*. New York: Riverhead Books, 1996.

Rupp, Joyce. *Praying Our Goodbyes*. Notre Dame, IN: Ave Maria Press, 1988.

Vogt, Eric E., Juanita Brown, and David Isaacs. "The Art of Powerful Questions: Catalyzing Insight, Innovation and Action." www.theworld-cafe.com/articles/aopq.pdf

Inspiration

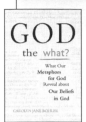

Finding Time for the Timeless: Spirituality in the Workweek
By John McQuiston II
Offers refreshing stories of everyday spiritual practices people use to free themselves from the work and worry mindset of our culture.
5⅛ x 6½, 208 pp, Quality PB, 978-1-59473-383-3 **$9.99**

God the *What?*: What Our Metaphors for God Reveal about Our Beliefs in God *by Carolyn Jane Bohler*
Inspires you to consider a wide range of images of God in order to refine how you imagine God. 6 x 9, 192 pp, Quality PB, 978-1-59473-251-5 **$16.99**

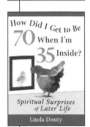

How Did I Get to Be 70 When I'm 35 Inside?: Spiritual Surprises of Later Life *by Linda Douty*
Encourages you to focus on the inner changes of aging to help you greet your later years as the grand adventure they can be. 6 x 9, 208 pp, Quality PB, 978-1-59473-297-3 **$16.99**

Restoring Life's Missing Pieces: The Spiritual Power of Remembering & Reuniting with People, Places, Things & Self *by Caren Goldman*
A powerful and thought-provoking look at reunions of all kinds as roads to remembering and re-membering ourselves.
6 x 9, 208 pp, Quality PB, 978-1-59473-295-9 **$16.99**

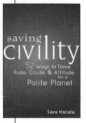

Saving Civility: 52 Ways to Tame Rude, Crude & Attitude for a Polite Planet
By Sara Hacala
Provides fifty-two practical ways you can reverse the course of incivility and make the world a more enriching, pleasant place to live.
6 x 9, 240 pp, Quality PB 978-1-59473-314-7 **$16.99**

Spiritually Healthy Divorce: Navigating Disruption with Insight & Hope
by Carolyne Call
A spiritual map to help you move through the twists and turns of divorce.
6 x 9, 224 pp, Quality PB, 978-1-59473-288-1 **$16.99**

Who Is My God? 2nd Edition
An Innovative Guide to Finding Your Spiritual Identity
by the Editors at SkyLight Paths
Provides the Spiritual Identity Self-Test™ to uncover the components of your unique spirituality. 6 x 9, 160 pp, Quality PB, 978-1-59473-014-6 **$15.99**

Journeys of Simplicity
Traveling Light with Thomas Merton, Bashō, Edward Abbey, Annie Dillard & Others
by Philip Harnden
Invites you to consider a more graceful way of traveling through life. PB includes journal pages to help you get started on your own spiritual journey.
5 x 7¼, 144 pp, Quality PB, 978-1-59473-181-5 **$12.99**
5 x 7¼, 128 pp, HC, 978-1-893361-76-8 **$16.95**

Or phone, fax, mail or e-mail to: SKYLIGHT PATHS Publishing
Sunset Farm Offices, Route 4 • P.O. Box 237 • Woodstock, Vermont 05091
Tel: (802) 457-4000 • Fax: (802) 457-4004 • www.skylightpaths.com
Credit card orders: (800) 962-4544 (8:30AM–5:30PM EST Monday–Friday)
Generous discounts on quantity orders. SATISFACTION GUARANTEED. Prices subject to change.

Children's Spirituality

ENDORSED BY CATHOLIC, PROTESTANT, JEWISH, AND BUDDHIST RELIGIOUS LEADERS

Adam & Eve's First Sunset: God's New Day
by Sandy Eisenberg Sasso; Full-color illus. by Joani Keller Rothenberg 9 x 12, 32 pp, Full-color illus.,
HC, 978-1-58023-177-0 **$17.95*** *For ages 4 & up*

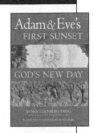

Because Nothing Looks Like God
by Lawrence Kushner and Karen Kushner; Full-color illus. by Dawn W. Majewski
Invites parents and children to explore the questions we all have about God.
11 x 8½, 32 pp, Full-color illus., HC, 978-1-58023-092-6 **$17.99*** *For ages 4 & up*
Also available: **Teacher's Guide** 8½ x 11, 22 pp, PB, 978-1-58023-140-4 **$6.95**

But God Remembered: Stories of Women from Creation to the
Promised Land *by Sandy Eisenberg Sasso; Full-color illus. by Bethanne Andersen*
A fascinating collection of four different stories of women only briefly mentioned in biblical tradition and religious texts.
9 x 12, 32 pp, Full-color illus., Quality PB, 978-1-58023-372-9 **$8.99*** *For ages 8 & up*

Cain & Abel: Finding the Fruits of Peace
by Sandy Eisenberg Sasso; Full-color illus. by Joani Keller Rothenberg
A sensitive recasting of the ancient tale shows we have the power to deal with anger in positive ways. "Editor's Choice." —American Library Association's *Booklist*
9 x 12, 32 pp, Full-color illus., HC, 978-1-58023-123-7 **$16.95*** *For ages 5 & up*

Does God Hear My Prayer?
by August Gold; Full-color photos by Diane Hardy Waller
Introduces preschoolers and young readers to prayer and how it helps them express their own emotions.
10 x 8½, 32 pp, Full-color photo illus., Quality PB, 978-1-59473-102-0 **$8.99** *For ages 3–6*

The 11th Commandment: Wisdom from Our Children *by The Children of America*
"If there were an Eleventh Commandment, what would it be?" Children of many religious denominations across America answer this question—in their own drawings and words. "A rare book of spiritual celebration for all people, of all ages, for all time." —*Bookviews* 8 x 10, 48 pp, Full-color illus., HC, 978-1-879045-46-0 **$16.95***
For all ages

For Heaven's Sake *by Sandy Eisenberg Sasso; Full-color illus. by Kathryn Kunz Finney*
Heaven is often found where you least expect it.
9 x 12, 32 pp, Full-color illus., HC, 978-1-58023-054-4 **$16.95*** *For ages 4 & up*

God in Between *by Sandy Eisenberg Sasso; Full-color illus. by Sally Sweetland*
A magical, mythical tale that teaches that God can be found where we are.
9 x 12, 32 pp, Full-color illus., HC, 978-1-879045-86-6 **$16.95*** *For ages 4 & up*

God's Paintbrush: Special 10th Anniversary Edition
by Sandy Eisenberg Sasso; Full-color illus. by Annette Compton
Invites children of all faiths and backgrounds to encounter God through moments in their own lives. 11 x 8½, 32 pp, Full-color illus., HC, 978-1-58023-195-4 **$17.95*** *For ages 4 & up*

Also available: **God's Paintbrush Teacher's Guide**
8½ x 11, 32 pp, PB, 978-1-879045-57-6 **$8.95**

God's Paintbrush Celebration Kit: A Spiritual Activity Kit for Teachers and
Students of All Faiths, All Backgrounds 9½ x 12, 40 Full-color Activity Sheets & Teacher Folder w/ complete instructions, HC, 978-1-58023-050-6 **$21.95**
Additional activity sheets available:
8-Student Activity Sheet Pack (40 sheets/5 sessions), 978-1-58023-058-2 **$19.95**
Single-Student Activity Sheet Pack (5 sessions), 978-1-58023-059-9 **$3.95**

I Am God's Paintbrush (A Board Book)
by Sandy Eisenberg Sasso; Full-color illus. by Annette Compton
5 x 5, 24 pp, Full-color illus., Board Book, 978-1-59473-265-2 **$7.99** *For ages 0–4*

* A book from Jewish Lights, SkyLight Paths' sister imprint

Sacred Texts—SkyLight Illuminations Series

Offers today's spiritual seeker an enjoyable entry into the great classic texts of the world's spiritual traditions. Each classic is presented in an accessible translation, with facing pages of guided commentary from experts, giving you the keys you need to understand the history, context and meaning of the text.

CHRISTIANITY

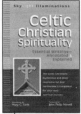

Celtic Christian Spirituality: Essential Writings—Annotated & Explained
Annotation by Mary C. Earle; Foreword by John Philip Newell
Explores how the writings of this lively tradition embody the gospel.
5½ x 8½, 176 pp, Quality PB, 978-1-59473-302-4 **$16.99**

Desert Fathers and Mothers: Early Christian Wisdom Sayings—
Annotated & Explained
Annotation by Christine Valters Paintner, PhD
Opens up wisdom of the desert fathers and mothers for readers with no previous knowledge of Western monasticism and early Christianity.
5½ x 8½, 192 pp, Quality PB, 978-1-59473-373-4 **$16.99**

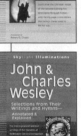

The End of Days: Essential Selections from Apocalyptic Texts—
Annotated & Explained
Annotation by Robert G. Clouse, PhD
Helps you understand the complex Christian visions of the end of the world.
5½ x 8½, 224 pp, Quality PB, 978-1-59473-170-9 **$16.99**

The Hidden Gospel of Matthew: Annotated & Explained
Translation & Annotation by Ron Miller
Discover the words and events that have the strongest connection to the historical Jesus.
5½ x 8½, 272 pp, Quality PB, 978-1-59473-038-2 **$16.99**

The Infancy Gospels of Jesus: Apocryphal Tales from the Childhoods of Mary and Jesus—Annotated & Explained
Translation & Annotation by Stevan Davies; Foreword by A. Edward Siecienski, PhD
A startling presentation of the early lives of Mary, Jesus and other biblical figures that will amuse and surprise you.
5½ x 8½, 176 pp, Quality PB, 978-1-59473-258-4 **$16.99**

John & Charles Wesley: Selections from Their Writings and Hymns—
Annotated & Explained
Annotation by Paul W. Chilcote, PhD
A unique presentation of the writings of these two inspiring brothers brings together some of the most essential material from their large corpus of work.
5½ x 8½, 288 pp, Quality PB, 978-1-59473-309-3 **$16.99**

The Lost Sayings of Jesus: Teachings from Ancient Christian, Jewish, Gnostic and Islamic Sources—Annotated & Explained
Translation & Annotation by Andrew Phillip Smith; Foreword by Stephan A. Hoeller
This collection of more than three hundred sayings depicts Jesus as a Wisdom teacher who speaks to people of all faiths as a mystic and spiritual master.
5½ x 8½, 240 pp, Quality PB, 978-1-59473-172-3 **$16.99**

Philokalia: The Eastern Christian Spiritual Texts—Selections
Annotated & Explained *Annotation by Allyne Smith; Translation by G. E. H. Palmer, Phillip Sherrard and Bishop Kallistos Ware*
The first approachable introduction to the wisdom of the Philokalia, the classic text of Eastern Christian spirituality.
5½ x 8½, 240 pp, Quality PB, 978-1-59473-103-7 **$16.99**

The Sacred Writings of Paul: Selections Annotated & Explained
Translation & Annotation by Ron Miller
Leads you into the exciting immediacy of Paul's teachings.
5½ x 8½, 224 pp, Quality PB, 978-1-59473-213-3 **$16.99**

Sacred Texts—continued

CHRISTIANITY—continued

Saint Augustine of Hippo: Selections from *Confessions* and Other Essential Writings—Annotated & Explained
Annotation by Joseph T. Kelley, PhD; Translation by the Augustinian Heritage Institute
Provides insight into the mind and heart of this foundational Christian figure.
5½ x 8½, 272 pp, Quality PB, 978-1-59473-282-9 **$16.99**

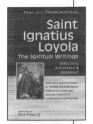

Saint Ignatius Loyola—The Spiritual Writings: Selections
Annotated & Explained *Annotation by Mark Mossa, SJ*
Draws from contemporary translations of original texts focusing on the practical mysticism of Ignatius of Loyola.
5½ x 8½, 288 pp, Quality PB, 978-1-59473-301-7 **$16.99**

Sex Texts from the Bible: Selections Annotated & Explained
Translation & Annotation by Teresa J. Hornsby; Foreword by Amy-Jill Levine
Demystifies the Bible's ideas on gender roles, marriage, sexual orientation, virginity, lust and sexual pleasure.
5½ x 8½, 208 pp, Quality PB, 978-1-59473-217-1 **$16.99**

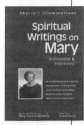

Spiritual Writings on Mary: Annotated & Explained
Annotation by Mary Ford-Grabowsky; Foreword by Andrew Harvey
Examines the role of Mary, the mother of Jesus, as a source of inspiration in history and in life today.
5½ x 8½, 288 pp, Quality PB, 978-1-59473-001-6 **$16.99**

The Way of a Pilgrim: The Jesus Prayer Journey—Annotated & Explained
Translation & Annotation by Gleb Pokrovsky; Foreword by Andrew Harvey
A classic of Russian Orthodox spirituality.
5½ x 8½, 160 pp, Illus., Quality PB, 978-1-893361-31-7 **$14.95**

GNOSTICISM

Gnostic Writings on the Soul: Annotated & Explained
Translation & Annotation by Andrew Phillip Smith; Foreword by Stephan A. Hoeller
Reveals the inspiring ways your soul can remember and return to its unique, divine purpose.
5½ x 8½, 144 pp, Quality PB, 978-1-59473-220-1 **$16.99**

The Gospel of Philip: Annotated & Explained
Translation & Annotation by Andrew Phillip Smith; Foreword by Stevan Davies
Reveals otherwise unrecorded sayings of Jesus and fragments of Gnostic mythology.
5½ x 8½, 160 pp, Quality PB, 978-1-59473-111-2 **$16.99**

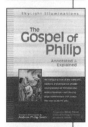

The Gospel of Thomas: Annotated & Explained
Translation & Annotation by Stevan Davies; Foreword by Andrew Harvey
Sheds new light on the origins of Christianity and portrays Jesus as a wisdom-loving sage.
5½ x 8½, 192 pp, Quality PB, 978-1-893361-45-4 **$16.99**

The Secret Book of John: The Gnostic Gospel—Annotated & Explained
Translation & Annotation by Stevan Davies
The most significant and influential text of the ancient Gnostic religion.
5½ x 8½, 208 pp, Quality PB, 978-1-59473-082-5 **$16.99**

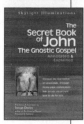

Bible Stories / Folktales

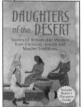

Abraham's Bind & Other Bible Tales of Trickery, Folly, Mercy and Love by Michael J. Caduto
New retellings of episodes in the lives of familiar biblical characters explore relevant life lessons. 6 x 9, 224 pp, HC, 978-1-59473-186-0 **$19.99**

Daughters of the Desert: Stories of Remarkable Women from Christian, Jewish and Muslim Traditions by Claire Rudolf Murphy,
Meghan Nuttall Sayres, Mary Cronk Farrell, Sarah Conover and Betsy Wharton
Breathes new life into the old tales of our female ancestors in faith. Uses traditional scriptural passages as starting points, then with vivid detail fills in historical context and place. Chapters reveal the voices of Sarah, Hagar, Huldah, Esther, Salome, Mary Magdalene, Lydia, Khadija, Fatima and many more. Historical fiction ideal for readers of all ages.
5½ x 8½, 192 pp, Quality PB, 978-1-59473-106-8 **$14.99** Inc. reader's discussion guide
HC, 978-1-893361-72-0 **$19.95**

The Triumph of Eve & Other Subversive Bible Tales
by Matt Biers-Ariel
These engaging retellings of familiar Bible stories are witty, often hilarious and always profound. They invite you to grapple with questions and issues that are often hidden in the original texts.
5½ x 8½, 192 pp, Quality PB, 978-1-59473-176-1 **$14.99**

Also available: **The Triumph of Eve Teacher's Guide**
8½ x 11, 44 pp, PB, 978-1-59473-152-5 **$8.99**

Wisdom in the Telling
Finding Inspiration and Grace in Traditional Folktales and Myths Retold
by Lorraine Hartin-Gelardi
6 x 9, 192 pp, HC, 978-1-59473-185-3 **$19.99**

Religious Etiquette / Reference

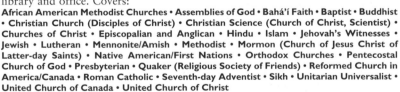

How to Be a Perfect Stranger, 5th Edition: The Essential Religious Etiquette Handbook Edited by Stuart M. Matlins and Arthur J. Magida
The indispensable guidebook to help the well-meaning guest when visiting other people's religious ceremonies. A straightforward guide to the rituals and celebrations of the major religions and denominations in the United States and Canada from the perspective of an interested guest of any other faith, based on information obtained from authorities of each religion. Belongs in every living room, library and office. Covers:

African American Methodist Churches • Assemblies of God • Bahá'í Faith • Baptist • Buddhist • Christian Church (Disciples of Christ) • Christian Science (Church of Christ, Scientist) • Churches of Christ • Episcopalian and Anglican • Hindu • Islam • Jehovah's Witnesses • Jewish • Lutheran • Mennonite/Amish • Methodist • Mormon (Church of Jesus Christ of Latter-day Saints) • Native American/First Nations • Orthodox Churches • Pentecostal Church of God • Presbyterian • Quaker (Religious Society of Friends) • Reformed Church in America/Canada • Roman Catholic • Seventh-day Adventist • Sikh • Unitarian Universalist • United Church of Canada • United Church of Christ

"The things Miss Manners forgot to tell us about religion."

—*Los Angeles Times*

"Finally, for those inclined to undertake their own spiritual journeys ... tells visitors what to expect." —*New York Times*

6 x 9, 432 pp, Quality PB, 978-1-59473-294-2 **$19.99**

The Perfect Stranger's Guide to Funerals and Grieving Practices: A Guide
to Etiquette in Other People's Religious Ceremonies Edited by Stuart M. Matlins
6 x 9, 240 pp, Quality PB, 978-1-893361-20-1 **$16.95**

The Perfect Stranger's Guide to Wedding Ceremonies: A Guide to
Etiquette in Other People's Religious Ceremonies Edited by Stuart M. Matlins
6 x 9, 208 pp, Quality PB, 978-1-893361-19-5 **$16.95**

Spiritual Poetry—The Mystic Poets

Experience these mystic poets as you never have before. Each beautiful, compact book includes a brief introduction to the poet's time and place, a summary of the major themes of the poet's mysticism and religious tradition, essential selections from the poet's most important works, and an appreciative preface by a contemporary spiritual writer.

Hafiz
The Mystic Poets
Translated and with Notes by Gertrude Bell
Preface by Ibrahim Gamard

Hafiz is known throughout the world as Persia's greatest poet, with sales of his poems in Iran today only surpassed by those of the Qur'an itself. His probing and joyful verse speaks to people from all backgrounds who long to taste and feel divine love and experience harmony with all living things.
5 x 7¼, 144 pp, HC, 978-1-59473-009-2 **$16.99**

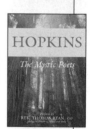

Hopkins
The Mystic Poets
Preface by Rev. Thomas Ryan, CSP

Gerard Manley Hopkins, Christian mystical poet, is beloved for his use of fresh language and startling metaphors to describe the world around him. Although his verse is lovely, beneath the surface lies a searching soul, wrestling with and yearning for God.
5 x 7¼, 112 pp, HC, 978-1-59473-010-8 **$16.99**

Tagore
The Mystic Poets
Preface by Swami Adiswarananda

Rabindranath Tagore is often considered the Shakespeare of modern India. A great mystic, Tagore was the teacher of W. B. Yeats and Robert Frost, the close friend of Albert Einstein and Mahatma Gandhi, and the winner of the Nobel Prize for Literature. This beautiful sampling of Tagore's two most important works, *The Gardener* and *Gitanjali*, offers a glimpse into his spiritual vision that has inspired people around the world.
5 x 7¼, 144 pp, HC, 978-1-59473-008-5 **$16.99**

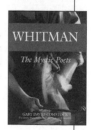

Whitman
The Mystic Poets
Preface by Gary David Comstock

Walt Whitman was the most innovative and influential poet of the nineteenth century. This beautiful sampling of Whitman's most important poetry from *Leaves of Grass*, and selections from his prose writings, offers a glimpse into the spiritual side of his most radical themes—love for country, love for others and love of self.
5 x 7¼, 192 pp, HC, 978-1-59473-041-2 **$16.99**

Spirituality of the Seasons

Autumn: A Spiritual Biography of the Season
Edited by Gary Schmidt and Susan M. Felch; Illus. by Mary Azarian
Rejoice in autumn as a time of preparation and reflection. Includes Wendell Berry, David James Duncan, Robert Frost, A. Bartlett Giamatti, E. B. White, P. D. James, Julian of Norwich, Garret Keizer, Tracy Kidder, Anne Lamott, May Sarton.
6 x 9, 320 pp, b/w illus., Quality PB, 978-1-59473-118-1 **$18.99**

Spring: A Spiritual Biography of the Season
Edited by Gary Schmidt and Susan M. Felch; Illus. by Mary Azarian
Explore the gentle unfurling of spring and reflect on how nature celebrates rebirth and renewal. Includes Jane Kenyon, Lucy Larcom, Harry Thurston, Nathaniel Hawthorne, Noel Perrin, Annie Dillard, Martha Ballard, Barbara Kingsolver, Dorothy Wordsworth, Donald Hall, David Brill, Lionel Basney, Isak Dinesen, Paul Laurence Dunbar. 6 x 9, 352 pp, b/w illus., Quality PB, 978-1-59473-246-1 **$18.99**

Summer: A Spiritual Biography of the Season
Edited by Gary Schmidt and Susan M. Felch; Illus. by Barry Moser
"A sumptuous banquet.... These selections lift up an exquisite wholeness found within an everyday sophistication." — ★ *Publishers Weekly* starred review
Includes Anne Lamott, Luci Shaw, Ray Bradbury, Richard Selzer, Thomas Lynch, Walt Whitman, Carl Sandburg, Sherman Alexie, Madeleine L'Engle, Jamaica Kincaid.
6 x 9, 304 pp, b/w illus., Quality PB, 978-1-59473-183-9 **$18.99**
HC, 978-1-59473-083-2 **$21.99**

Winter: A Spiritual Biography of the Season
Edited by Gary Schmidt and Susan M. Felch; Illus. by Barry Moser
"This outstanding anthology features top-flight nature and spirituality writers on the fierce, inexorable season of winter.... Remarkably lively and warm, despite the icy subject." — ★ *Publishers Weekly* starred review
Includes Will Campbell, Rachel Carson, Annie Dillard, Donald Hall, Ron Hansen, Jane Kenyon, Jamaica Kincaid, Barry Lopez, Kathleen Norris, John Updike, E. B. White.
6 x 9, 288 pp, b/w illus., Deluxe PB w/ flaps, 978-1-893361-92-8 **$18.95**
HC, 978-1-893361-53-9 **$21.95**

Spirituality / Animal Companions

Blessing the Animals: Prayers and Ceremonies to Celebrate God's Creatures, Wild and Tame *Edited and with Introductions by Lynn L. Caruso*
5¼ x 7¼, 256 pp, Quality PB, 978-1-59473-253-9 **$15.99**; HC, 978-1-59473-145-7 **$19.99**

Remembering My Pet: A Kid's Own Spiritual Workbook for When a Pet Dies
by Nechama Liss-Levinson, PhD, and Rev. Molly Phinney Baskette, MDiv; Foreword by Lynn L. Caruso
8 x 10, 48 pp, 2-color text, HC, 978-1-59473-221-8 **$16.99**

What Animals Can Teach Us about Spirituality: Inspiring Lessons from Wild and Tame Creatures *by Diana L. Guerrero* 6 x 9, 176 pp, Quality PB, 978-1-893361-84-3 **$16.95**

Spirituality—A Week Inside

Lighting the Lamp of Wisdom: A Week Inside a Yoga Ashram
by John Ittner; Foreword by Dr. David Frawley
6 x 9, 192 pp, b/w photos, Quality PB, 978-1-893361-52-2 **$15.95**

Making a Heart for God: A Week Inside a Catholic Monastery
by Dianne Aprile; Foreword by Brother Patrick Hart, OCSO
6 x 9, 224 pp, b/w photos, Quality PB, 978-1-893361-49-2 **$16.95**

Waking Up: A Week Inside a Zen Monastery
by Jack Maguire; Foreword by John Daido Loori, Roshi
6 x 9, 224 pp, b/w photos, Quality PB, 978-1-893361-55-3 **$16.95**; HC, 978-1-893361-13-3 **$21.95**

Spirituality

Gathering at God's Table: The Meaning of Mission in the Feast of Faith
By Katharine Jefferts Schori
A profound reminder of our role in the larger frame of God's dream for a restored and reconciled world. 6 x 9, 256 pp, HC, 978-1-59473-316-1 **$21.99**

The Heartbeat of God: Finding the Sacred in the Middle of Everything
by Katharine Jefferts Schori; Foreword by Joan Chittister, OSB
Explores our connections to other people, to other nations and with the environment through the lens of faith. 6 x 9, 240 pp, HC, 978-1-59473-292-8 **$21.99**

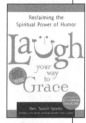

A Dangerous Dozen: Twelve Christians Who Threatened the Status Quo but Taught Us to Live Like Jesus
by the Rev. Canon C. K. Robertson, PhD; Foreword by Archbishop Desmond Tutu
Profiles twelve visionary men and women who challenged society and showed the world a different way of living. 6 x 9, 208 pp, Quality PB, 978-1-59473-298-0 **$16.99**

Decision Making & Spiritual Discernment: The Sacred Art of Finding Your Way *by Nancy L. Bieber*
Presents three essential aspects of Spirit-led decision making: willingness, attentiveness and responsiveness. 5½ x 8½, 208 pp, Quality PB, 978-1-59473-289-8 **$16.99**

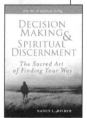

Laugh Your Way to Grace: Reclaiming the Spiritual Power of Humor
by Rev. Susan Sparks A powerful, humorous case for laughter as a spiritual, healing path. 6 x 9, 176 pp, Quality PB, 978-1-59473-280-5 **$16.99**

Bread, Body, Spirit: Finding the Sacred in Food
Edited and with Introductions by Alice Peck 6 x 9, 224 pp, Quality PB, 978-1-59473-242-3 **$19.99**

Claiming Earth as Common Ground: The Ecological Crisis through the Lens of Faith
by Andrea Cohen-Kiener; Foreword by Rev. Sally Bingham
6 x 9, 192 pp, Quality PB, 978-1-59473-261-4 **$16.99**

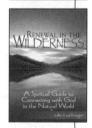

Creating a Spiritual Retirement: A Guide to the Unseen Possibilities in Our Lives
by Molly Srode 6 x 9, 208 pp, b/w photos, Quality PB, 978-1-59473-050-4 **$14.99**

Creative Aging: Rethinking Retirement and Non-Retirement in a Changing World
by Marjory Zoet Bankson 6 x 9, 160 pp, Quality PB, 978-1-59473-281-2 **$16.99**

Keeping Spiritual Balance as We Grow Older: More than 65 Creative Ways to Use Purpose, Prayer, and the Power of Spirit to Build a Meaningful Retirement
by Molly and Bernie Srode 8 x 8, 224 pp, Quality PB, 978-1-59473-042-9 **$16.99**

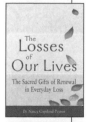

Hearing the Call across Traditions: Readings on Faith and Service
Edited by Adam Davis; Foreword by Eboo Patel
6 x 9, 352 pp, Quality PB, 978-1-59473-303-1 **$18.99**; HC, 978-1-59473-264-5 **$29.99**

Honoring Motherhood: Prayers, Ceremonies & Blessings
Edited and with Introductions by Lynn L. Caruso
5 x 7¼, 272 pp, Quality PB, 978-1-58473-384-0 **$9.99**; HC, 978-1-59473-239-3 **$19.99**

The Losses of Our Lives: The Sacred Gifts of Renewal in Everyday Loss
by Dr. Nancy Copeland-Payton 6 x 9, 192 pp, HC, 978-1-59473-271-3 **$19.99**

Renewal in the Wilderness: A Spiritual Guide to Connecting with God in the Natural World *by John Lionberger*
6 x 9, 176 pp, b/w photos, Quality PB, 978-1-59473-219-5 **$16.99**

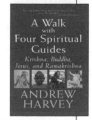

Soul Fire: Accessing Your Creativity
by Thomas Ryan, CSP 6 x 9, 160 pp, Quality PB, 978-1-59473-243-0 **$16.99**

A Spirituality for Brokenness: Discovering Your Deepest Self in Difficult Times
by Terry Taylor 6 x 9, 176 pp, Quality PB, 978-1-59473-229-4 **$16.99**

A Walk with Four Spiritual Guides: Krishna, Buddha, Jesus, and Ramakrishna
by Andrew Harvey 5½ x 8½, 192 pp, b/w photos & illus., Quality PB, 978-1-59473-138-9 **$15.99**

The Workplace and Spirituality: New Perspectives on Research and Practice
Edited by Dr. Joan Marques, Dr. Satinder Dhiman and Dr. Richard King
6 x 9, 256 pp, HC, 978-1-59473-260-7 **$29.99**

Spirituality & Crafts

Beading—The Creative Spirit: Finding Your Sacred Center through the Art of Beadwork *by Rev. Wendy Ellsworth*
Invites you on a spiritual pilgrimage into the kaleidoscope world of glass and color. 7 x 9, 240 pp, 8-page color insert, 40+ b/w photos and 40 diagrams, Quality PB, 978-1-59473-267-6 **$18.99**

Contemplative Crochet: A Hands-On Guide for Interlocking Faith and Craft *by Cindy Crandall-Frazier; Foreword by Linda Skolnik*
Illuminates the spiritual lessons you can learn through crocheting.
7 x 9, 208 pp, b/w photos, Quality PB, 978-1-59473-238-6 **$16.99**

The Knitting Way: A Guide to Spiritual Self-Discovery
by Linda Skolnik and Janice MacDaniels Examines how you can explore and strengthen your spiritual life through knitting.
7 x 9, 240 pp, b/w photos, Quality PB, 978-1-59473-079-5 **$16.99**

The Painting Path: Embodying Spiritual Discovery through Yoga, Brush and Color *by Linda Novick; Foreword by Richard Segalman*
Explores the divine connection you can experience through art.
7 x 9, 208 pp, 8-page color insert, plus b/w photos,
Quality PB, 978-1-59473-226-3 **$18.99**

The Quilting Path: A Guide to Spiritual Discovery through Fabric, Thread and Kabbalah *by Louise Silk*
Explores how to cultivate personal growth through quilt making.
7 x 9, 192 pp, b/w photos and illus., Quality PB, 978-1-59473-206-5 **$16.99**

The Scrapbooking Journey: A Hands-On Guide to Spiritual Discovery
by Cory Richardson-Lauve; Foreword by Stacy Julian Reveals how this craft can become a practice used to deepen and shape your life.
7 x 9, 176 pp, 8-page color insert, plus b/w photos, Quality PB, 978-1-59473-216-4 **$18.99**

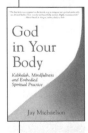

The Soulwork of Clay: A Hands-On Approach to Spirituality
by Marjory Zoet Bankson; Photos by Peter Bankson
Takes you through the seven-step process of making clay into a pot, drawing parallels at each stage to the process of spiritual growth.
7 x 9, 192 pp, b/w photos, Quality PB, 978-1-59473-249-2 **$16.99**

Kabbalah / Enneagram
(Books from Jewish Lights Publishing, SkyLight Paths' sister imprint)

Cast in God's Image: Discover Your Personality Type Using the Enneagram and Kabbalah
by Rabbi Howard A. Addison, PhD 7 x 9, 176 pp, Quality PB, 978-1-58023-124-4 **$16.95**

Ehyeh: A Kabbalah for Tomorrow *by Rabbi Arthur Green, PhD*
6 x 9, 224 pp, Quality PB, 978-1-58023-213-5 **$18.99**

The Enneagram and Kabbalah, 2nd Edition: Reading Your Soul
by Rabbi Howard A. Addison, PhD 6 x 9, 192 pp, Quality PB, 978-1-58023-229-6 **$16.99**

The Gift of Kabbalah: Discovering the Secrets of Heaven, Renewing Your Life on Earth
by Tamar Frankiel, PhD 6 x 9, 256 pp, Quality PB, 978-1-58023-141-1 **$16.95**

God in Your Body: Kabbalah, Mindfulness and Embodied Spiritual Practice
by Jay Michaelson 6 x 9, 272 pp, Quality PB, 978-1-58023-304-0 **$18.99**

Jewish Mysticism and the Spiritual Life: Classical Texts, Contemporary Reflections
Edited by Dr. Lawrence Fine, Dr. Eitan Fishbane and Rabbi Or N. Rose
6 x 9, 256 pp, HC, 978-1-58023-434-4 **$24.99**

Kabbalah: A Brief Introduction for Christians
by Tamar Frankiel, PhD 5½ x 8½, 208 pp, Quality PB, 978-1-58023-303-3 **$16.99**

Zohar: Annotated & Explained *Translation & Annotation by Daniel C. Matt; Foreword by Andrew Harvey* 5½ x 8½, 176 pp, Quality PB, 978-1-893361-51-5 **$15.99**

Spiritual Practice

Fly-Fishing—The Sacred Art: Casting a Fly as a Spiritual Practice
by Rabbi Eric Eisenkramer and Rev. Michael Attas, MD; Foreword by Chris Wood, CEO,
Trout Unlimited; Preface by Lori Simon, executive director, Casting for Recovery
Shares what fly-fishing can teach you about reflection, awe and wonder; the benefits
of solitude; the blessing of community and the search for the Divine.
5½ x 8½, 160 pp, Quality PB, 978-1-59473-299-7 **$16.99**

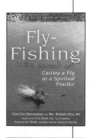

Lectio Divina—The Sacred Art: Transforming Words & Images into
Heart-Centered Prayer *by Christine Valters Paintner, PhD*
Expands the practice of sacred reading beyond scriptural texts and makes it
accessible in contemporary life. 5½ x 8½, 240 pp, Quality PB, 978-1-59473-300-0 **$16.99**

Writing—The Sacred Art: Beyond the Page to Spiritual Practice
By Rami Shapiro and Aaron Shapiro
Push your writing through the trite and the boring to something fresh, something
transformative. Includes over fifty unique, practical exercises.
5½ x 8½, 192 pp, Quality PB, 978-1-59473-372-7 **$16.99**

Dance—The Sacred Art: The Joy of Movement as a Spiritual Practice
by Cynthia Winton-Henry 5½ x 8½, 224 pp, Quality PB, 978-1-59473-268-3 **$16.99**

Everyday Herbs in Spiritual Life: A Guide to Many Practices
by Michael J. Caduto; Foreword by Rosemary Gladstar
7 x 9, 208 pp, 20+ b/w illus., Quality PB, 978-1-59473-174-7 **$16.99**

Giving—The Sacred Art: Creating a Lifestyle of Generosity
by Lauren Tyler Wright 5½ x 8½, 208 pp, Quality PB, 978-1-59473-224-9 **$16.99**

Haiku—The Sacred Art: A Spiritual Practice in Three Lines
by Margaret D. McGee 5½ x 8½, 192 pp, Quality PB, 978-1-59473-269-0 **$16.99**

Hospitality—The Sacred Art: Discovering the Hidden Spiritual Power of Invitation
and Welcome *by Rev. Nanette Sawyer; Foreword by Rev. Dirk Ficca*
5½ x 8½, 208 pp, Quality PB, 978-1-59473-228-7 **$16.99**

Labyrinths from the Outside In: Walking to Spiritual Insight—A Beginner's Guide
by Donna Schaper and Carole Ann Camp
6 x 9, 208 pp, b/w illus. and photos, Quality PB, 978-1-893361-18-8 **$16.95**

Practicing the Sacred Art of Listening: A Guide to Enrich Your Relationships
and Kindle Your Spiritual Life *by Kay Lindahl* 8 x 8, 176 pp, Quality PB, 978-1-893361-85-0 **$16.95**

Recovery—The Sacred Art: The Twelve Steps as Spiritual Practice *by Rami Shapiro;*
Foreword by Joan Borysenko, PhD 5½ x 8½, 240 pp, Quality PB, 978-1-59473-259-1 **$16.99**

Running—The Sacred Art: Preparing to Practice *by Dr. Warren A. Kay; Foreword by*
Kristin Armstrong 5½ x 8½, 160 pp, Quality PB, 978-1-59473-227-0 **$16.99**

The Sacred Art of Chant: Preparing to Practice
by Ana Hernández 5½ x 8½, 192 pp, Quality PB, 978-1-59473-036-8 **$15.99**

The Sacred Art of Fasting: Preparing to Practice
by Thomas Ryan, CSP 5½ x 8½, 192 pp, Quality PB, 978-1-59473-078-8 **$15.99**

The Sacred Art of Forgiveness: Forgiving Ourselves and Others through God's Grace
by Marcia Ford 8 x 8, 176 pp, Quality PB, 978-1-59473-175-4 **$18.99**

The Sacred Art of Listening: Forty Reflections for Cultivating a Spiritual Practice
by Kay Lindahl; Illus. by Amy Schnapper 8 x 8, 160 pp, b/w illus., Quality PB, 978-1-893361-44-7 **$16.99**

The Sacred Art of Lovingkindness: Preparing to Practice
by Rabbi Rami Shapiro; Foreword by Marcia Ford 5½ x 8½, 176 pp, Quality PB, 978-1-59473-151-8 **$16.99**

Sacred Attention: A Spiritual Practice for Finding God in the Moment
by Margaret D. McGee 6 x 9, 144 pp, Quality PB, 978-1-59473-291-1 **$16.99**

Soul Fire: Accessing Your Creativity
by Thomas Ryan, CSP 6 x 9, 160 pp, Quality PB, 978-1-59473-243-0 **$16.99**

Spiritual Adventures in the Snow: Skiing & Snowboarding as Renewal for Your Soul
by Dr. Marcia McFee and Rev. Karen Foster; Foreword by Paul Arthur
5½ x 8½, 208 pp, Quality PB, 978-1-59473-270-6 **$16.99**

Thanking & Blessing—The Sacred Art: Spiritual Vitality through Gratefulness
by Jay Marshall, PhD; Foreword by Philip Gulley 5½ x 8½, 176 pp, Quality PB, 978-1-59473-231-7 **$16.99**

Women's Interest

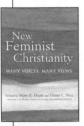

Women, Spirituality and Transformative Leadership
Where Grace Meets Power
Edited by Kathe Schaaf, Kay Lindahl, Kathleen S. Hurty, PhD, and Reverend Guo Cheen
A dynamic conversation on the power of women's spiritual leadership and its emerging patterns of transformation. 6 x 9, 288 pp, Hardcover, 978-1-59473-313-0 **$24.99**

Spiritually Healthy Divorce: Navigating Disruption with Insight & Hope
by Carolyne Call A spiritual map to help you move through the twists and turns of divorce. 6 x 9, 224 pp, Quality PB, 978-1-59473-288-1 **$16.99**

New Feminist Christianity: Many Voices, Many Views
Edited by Mary E. Hunt and Diann L. Neu
Insights from ministers and theologians, activists and leaders, artists and liturgists who are shaping the future. Taken together, their voices offer a starting point for building new models of religious life and worship.
6 x 9, 384 pp, HC, 978-1-59473-285-0 **$24.99**

New Jewish Feminism: Probing the Past, Forging the Future
Edited by Rabbi Elyse Goldstein; Foreword by Anita Diamant
Looks at the growth and accomplishments of Jewish feminism and what they mean for Jewish women today and tomorrow. Features the voices of women from every area of Jewish life, addressing the important issues that concern Jewish women.
6 x 9, 480 pp, Quality PB, 978-1-58023-448-1 **$19.99**; HC, 978-1-58023-359-0 **$24.99***

Bread, Body, Spirit: Finding the Sacred in Food
Edited and with Introductions by Alice Peck 6 x 9, 224 pp, Quality PB, 978-1-59473-242-3 **$19.99**

Dance—The Sacred Art: The Joy of Movement as a Spiritual Practice
by Cynthia Winton-Henry 5½ x 8½, 224 pp, Quality PB, 978-1-59473-268-3 **$16.99**

Daughters of the Desert: Stories of Remarkable Women from Christian, Jewish and Muslim Traditions
by Claire Rudolf Murphy, Meghan Nuttall Sayres, Mary Cronk Farrell, Sarah Conover and Betsy Wharton 5½ x 8½, 192 pp, Illus., Quality PB, 978-1-59473-106-8 **$14.99** Inc. reader's discussion guide

The Divine Feminine in Biblical Wisdom Literature
Selections Annotated & Explained
Translation & Annotation by Rabbi Rami Shapiro; Foreword by Rev. Cynthia Bourgeault, PhD
5½ x 8½, 240 pp, Quality PB, 978-1-59473-109-9 **$16.99**

Divining the Body: Reclaim the Holiness of Your Physical Self
by Jan Phillips 8 x 8, 256 pp, Quality PB, 978-1-59473-080-1 **$18.99**

Honoring Motherhood: Prayers, Ceremonies & Blessings
Edited and with Introductions by Lynn L. Caruso
5 x 7¼, 272 pp, Quality PB, 978-1-58473-384-0 **$9.99**; HC, 978-1-59473-239-3 **$19.99**

Next to Godliness: Finding the Sacred in Housekeeping
Edited by Alice Peck 6 x 9, 224 pp, Quality PB, 978-1-59473-214-0 **$19.99**

ReVisions: Seeing Torah through a Feminist Lens
by Rabbi Elyse Goldstein 5½ x 8½, 224 pp, Quality PB, 978-1-58023-117-6 **$16.95***

The Triumph of Eve & Other Subversive Bible Tales
by Matt Biers-Ariel 5½ x 8½, 192 pp, Quality PB, 978-1-59473-176-1 **$14.99**

White Fire: A Portrait of Women Spiritual Leaders in America
by Malka Drucker; Photos by Gay Block 7 x 10, 320 pp, b/w photos, HC, 978-1-893361-64-5 **$24.95**

Woman Spirit Awakening in Nature: Growing Into the Fullness of Who You Are
by Nancy Barrett Chickerneo, PhD; Foreword by Eileen Fisher
8 x 8, 224 pp, b/w illus., Quality PB, 978-1-59473-250-8 **$16.99**

Women of Color Pray: Voices of Strength, Faith, Healing, Hope and Courage
Edited and with Introductions by Christal M. Jackson
5 x 7¼, 208 pp, Quality PB, 978-1-59473-077-1 **$15.99**

The Women's Torah Commentary: New Insights from Women Rabbis on the 54 Weekly Torah Portions
Edited by Rabbi Elyse Goldstein
6 x 9, 496 pp, Quality PB, 978-1-58023-370-5 **$19.99**; HC, 978-1-58023-076-6 **$34.95***

* A book from Jewish Lights, SkyLight Paths' sister imprint

Prayer / Meditation

Men Pray: Voices of Strength, Faith, Healing, Hope and Courage
Created by the Editors at SkyLight Paths
Celebrates the rich variety of ways men around the world have called out to the Divine—with words of joy, praise, gratitude, wonder, petition and even anger—from the ancient world up to our own day.
5 x 7, 200 pp (est), HC, 978-1-59473-395-6 **$16.99**

Sacred Attention: A Spiritual Practice for Finding God in the Moment
by Margaret D. McGee
Framed on the Christian liturgical year, this inspiring guide explores ways to develop a practice of attention as a means of talking—and listening—to God.
6 x 9, 144 pp, Quality PB, 978-1-59473-291-1 **$16.99**

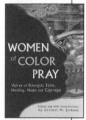

Women of Color Pray: Voices of Strength, Faith, Healing, Hope and Courage
Edited and with Introductions by Christal M. Jackson
Through these prayers, poetry, lyrics, meditations and affirmations, you will share in the strong and undeniable connection women of color share with God.
5 x 7¼, 208 pp, Quality PB, 978-1-59473-077-1 **$15.99**

The Art of Public Prayer, 2nd Edition: Not for Clergy Only
by Lawrence A. Hoffman, PhD 6 x 9, 288 pp, Quality PB, 978-1-893361-06-5 **$19.99**

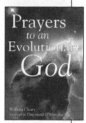

A Heart of Stillness: A Complete Guide to Learning the Art of Meditation
by David A. Cooper 5½ x 8½, 272 pp, Quality PB, 978-1-893361-03-4 **$18.99**

Living into Hope: A Call to Spiritual Action for Such a Time as This
by Rev. Dr. Joan Brown Campbell; Foreword by Karen Armstrong
6 x 9, 208 pp, HC, 978-1-59473-283-6 **$21.99**

Meditation without Gurus: A Guide to the Heart of Practice
by Clark Strand 5½ x 8½, 192 pp, Quality PB, 978-1-893361-93-5 **$16.95**

Prayers to an Evolutionary God
by William Cleary; Afterword by Diarmuid O'Murchu
6 x 9, 208 pp, HC, 978-1-59473-006-1 **$21.99**

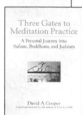

Praying with Our Hands: 21 Practices of Embodied Prayer from the World's Spiritual Traditions *by Jon M. Sweeney; Photos by Jennifer J. Wilson; Foreword by Mother Tessa Bielecki; Afterword by Taitetsu Unno, PhD*
8 x 8, 96 pp, 22 duotone photos, Quality PB, 978-1-893361-16-4 **$16.95**

Secrets of Prayer: A Multifaith Guide to Creating Personal Prayer in Your Life
by Nancy Corcoran, CSJ
6 x 9, 160 pp, Quality PB, 978-1-59473-215-7 **$16.99**

Three Gates to Meditation Practice: A Personal Journey into Sufism, Buddhism, and Judaism *by David A. Cooper* 5½ x 8½, 240 pp, Quality PB, 978-1-893361-22-5 **$16.95**

Prayer / M. Basil Pennington, OCSO

Finding Grace at the Center, 3rd Edition: The Beginning of Centering Prayer *with Thomas Keating, OCSO, and Thomas E. Clarke, SJ; Foreword by Rev. Cynthia Bourgeault, PhD* A practical guide to a simple and beautiful form of meditative prayer. 5 x 7¼,128 pp, Quality PB, 978-1-59473-182-2 **$12.99**

The Monks of Mount Athos: A Western Monk's Extraordinary Spiritual Journey on Eastern Holy Ground *Foreword by Archimandrite Dionysios*
Explores the landscape, monastic communities and food of Athos.
6 x 9, 352 pp, Quality PB, 978-1-893361-78-2 **$18.95**

Psalms: A Spiritual Commentary *Illus. by Phillip Ratner*
Reflections on some of the most beloved passages from the Bible's most widely read book. 6 x 9, 176 pp, 24 full-page b/w illus., Quality PB, 978-1-59473-234-8 **$16.99**

The Song of Songs: A Spiritual Commentary *Illus. by Phillip Ratner*
Explore the Bible's most challenging mystical text.
6 x 9, 160 pp, 14 full-page b/w illus., Quality PB, 978-1-59473-235-5 **$16.99**
HC, 978-1-59473-004-7 **$19.99**

About SKYLIGHT PATHS Publishing

SkyLight Paths Publishing is creating a place where people of different spiritual traditions come together for challenge and inspiration, a place where we can help each other understand the mystery that lies at the heart of our existence.

Through spirituality, our religious beliefs are increasingly becoming a part of our lives—rather than *apart* from our lives. While many of us may be more interested than ever in spiritual growth, we may be less firmly planted in traditional religion. Yet, we do want to deepen our relationship to the sacred, to learn from our own as well as from other faith traditions, and to practice in new ways.

SkyLight Paths sees both believers and seekers as a community that increasingly transcends traditional boundaries of religion and denomination—people wanting to learn from each other, *walking together, finding the way*.

For your information and convenience, at the back of this book we have provided a list of other SkyLight Paths books you might find interesting and useful. They cover the following subjects:

Buddhism / Zen	Global Spiritual	Monasticism
Catholicism	Perspectives	Mysticism
Children's Books	Gnosticism	Poetry
Christianity	Hinduism /	Prayer
Comparative	Vedanta	Religious Etiquette
Religion	Inspiration	Retirement
Current Events	Islam / Sufism	Spiritual Biography
Earth-Based	Judaism	Spiritual Direction
Spirituality	Kabbalah	Spirituality
Enneagram	Meditation	Women's Interest
	Midrash Fiction	Worship

Or phone, fax, mail or e-mail to: SKYLIGHT PATHS Publishing
Sunset Farm Offices, Route 4 • P.O. Box 237 • Woodstock, Vermont 05091
Tel: (802) 457-4000 • Fax: (802) 457-4004 • www.skylightpaths.com
Credit card orders: (800) 962-4544 (8:30AM–5:30PM EST Monday–Friday)
Generous discounts on quantity orders. SATISFACTION GUARANTEED. Prices subject to change.